Supervising and leading teams in ILS

Supervising and leading teams in ILS

Barbara Allan

facet publishing

Published by Facet Publishing
7 Ridgmount Street, London WC1E 7AE
www.facetpublishing.co.uk

Facet Publishing is wholly owned by CILIP: the Chartered Institute of
Library and Information Professionals.

First published 2007

British Library Cataloguing in Publication Data
A catalogue record for this book is available from the British Library.

ISBN-13: 978-1-85604-587-2
ISBN-10: 1-85604-587-0

Typeset in 10/13pt Revival 565 BT and Function by Facet Publishing.
Printed and made in Great Britain by MPG Books Ltd, Bodmin, Cornwall.

Contents

List of figures

List of tables

Acknowledgements

Many of the ideas and examples in this book have come from information and library workers whom I have met during workshops held at ALSIB/IMI and CILIP, and also through professional conferences. Thank you. I have changed your names and other details to maintain your anonymity and confidentiality. In addition, colleagues at the University of Hull and, in particular, the Hull University Business School have provided me with information and support during the writing of this book. I would like to thank David Bright for his help in checking the accuracy of Chapter 8.

Chapters 4 and 7 evolved from work I have previously had published in my book *Project Management* (Facet Publishing). Chapter 9 has drawn on ideas that I first presented in my book *Training Skills for Library and Information Workers* (Facet Publishing).

Finally, I would like to thank my husband, Denis, and daughter, Sarah, for their help and support during this project.

Introduction

The aim of this book is to provide a practical guide for new and aspiring team leaders and supervisors. The book covers the main areas of concern for new team leaders and supervisors, and it is also relevant to experienced practitioners who wish to refresh their approach to managing teams.

This book is based on information and knowledge obtained and developed from:

- my experiences as a team leader in academic and workplace information and library units
- my experiences in teamwork as an independent consultant and trainer
- feedback from colleagues attending my workshops run through professional associations such as CILIP and ASLIB/IMI in the UK
- visits (both real and virtual) to a wide range of information and library services (ILS)
- professional networks and conferences, and also the literature.

The book is not intended as a prescriptive guide to leading and supervising teams. It presents well tested and current approaches to teamwork and a range of examples and case studies, and these are meant to demonstrate current practice in a wide range of information and library units. After reading this book or dipping into it, I hope that you will use the tools and techniques that are most relevant to your professional context. Each topic is covered in a practical and down-to-earth manner. Although references are made to relevant theories the main focus of this book is on the practice of leading and supervising teams; it is very much a 'how to . . .' guide for supervisors and team leaders. Some chapters include self-assessment audits to enable you to consider and reflect upon your knowledge and skills. There are also a number of activities and the purpose of these is to help you to relate the content of each chapter to your own work situation. Individual chapters conclude with a list of references and the book ends with a guide to further reading and a brief index.

Chapter 1 provides an overview of working as a supervisor or team leader. This includes understanding the role and the responsibilities of team leaders and supervisors. This chapter includes an audit tool which you may use to reflect on and think about your knowledge and skills with respect to leading and supervising teams. Chapter 1 also provides a quick overview of the changing landscapes of ILS work and concludes with an overview of the strategic planning processes used in many organizations. This is important as team leaders and supervisors work within a strategic context and towards fulfilling an organization's strategic plan. Reading Chapter 1 will help you to understand the context of your work.

Chapter 2 provides an overview of managing the whole team. The main part of this chapter is concerned with providing a structured approach to managing the whole team. This is based around a series of questions relevant to both new and experienced team leaders. This is followed by a section that involves thinking about and understanding team development processes and different team roles. The final sections in this chapter consider the characteristics of effective team leaders and managers, and also the 'seven deadly sins' or the ways in which teams are demotivated and destroyed by weak or bad leadership or supervision.

Chapter 3 provides two approaches, the assertiveness model and the concept of emotional intelligence, that may be used as a way of developing a confident approach to leading and supervising teams. These models are explored in the context of teamwork with a number of practical examples and activities. This chapter includes an audit tool which you may use to reflect on and think about your own emotional intelligence. This is followed by a section on problem solving which provides a problem-solving methodology supported by a case study. This chapter concludes with a section on the management of change and this provides a framework to explain individual responses to changes within the workplace. It also suggests different ways in which team leaders can communicate with and lead their teams during the change process.

Chapter 4 is concerned with motivation and practical approaches to motivating individuals. This chapter briefly considers some psychological theories of motivation and relates them to information and library work through a case study. It also explores ways of understanding and motivating individuals and the whole team through the use of motivational traits.

Chapter 5 is concerned with managing the team's work and starts by considering the work environment. Most team leaders or supervisors are involved in managing the routine work of a team and this is explored in this chapter. Increasingly, team leaders and supervisors are also asked to take on project management so this section provides a quick overview of this topic. Finally, this chapter covers topics relevant to managing both the day-to-day work and also projects, i.e. delegating tasks, giving instructions, giving feedback, setting goals, and monitoring and reviewing performance.

Excellent communication skills are at the heart of leading and working with teams and this topic is covered in Chapter 6. Effective team leaders and supervisors think about the person to whom they are communicating, what they want to communicate, and also the most effective means of getting their message across. This chapter considers the following topics: briefing teams and individuals; leading meetings; listening skills; making presentations; and using e-mail and other virtual communication tools.

Many team leaders and supervisors are involved in managing one or more teams and these are sometimes complex teams, e.g. collaborative teams, multi-professional teams, diverse and international teams, and virtual teams. In addition, individual team members are likely to be members of more than one team. Working with and leading these complex teams is more challenging than leading a traditional team that deals with routine work and little change. Chapter 7 explores practical approaches to managing and leading different complex teams, and provides practical strategies that may be used to establish and develop effective teams. It includes a range of different case studies to illustrate some of the real-life situations that team leaders experience when working with complex teams.

Chapter 8 provides an overview of human resource management and covers the following topics: recruitment and selection; appraisal processes; performance management; disciplinary and grievance procedures; and equal opportunities and diversity. The key message in this chapter is that it is vital for team leaders and supervisors to gain professional advice and support when dealing with human-resource-management issues. The law and practice in this area are constantly changing so it is imperative that good quality and up-to-date advice is obtained at all times.

In recent years there has been a shift in emphasis from the idea of training and development to the concept of lifelong learning and continuous professional development (CPD). In Chapter 9 the focus is on workplace learning and this includes a wide range of learning activities such as training events. This chapter provides an overview of training and development, and the importance of identifying individual and team training needs. This chapter focuses on three specific examples of training and development that are likely to be experienced by many team leaders and supervisors, i.e. e-learning, coaching and learning through reflection.

Finally, Chapter 10 explores practical approaches to personal growth and development. This is vital if you are to provide effective team leadership or supervision particularly if you are working in a challenging and turbulent environment. This chapter covers the following topics: looking after yourself; work/life balance; time management; personal and career support; professional networks and communities of practice; and personal portfolios.

A guide to further reading and an index follow Chapter 10.

1   The role of team leaders in ILS

Introduction

This introductory chapter sets the context of leading and supervising teams in information and library services (ILS). The chapter discusses working as a team leader or supervisor; the role and the responsibilities; the context of library and information work; and the background to approaches to management including the strategic planning process.

Working as a team leader or supervisor

Working as a team leader or supervisor normally involves responsibility for a team plus their work. The team may be relatively small or large and may be located in one building or spread geographically across a country. Virtual teams are becoming increasingly common in ILS. Coming into the role of team leader for the first time may involve taking responsibility for an experienced team that has been established over a long period of time. It may involve working as a team leader with staff who perhaps applied for your position and were unsuccessful. Sometimes team leaders are appointed with the task of developing a new team from scratch. Case studies 1.1, 1.2 and 1.3 provide typical examples of team leaders in today's information and library world.

Case 1.1   Information work in a museum

Sam has taken up the role of team leader of a small team made up of two part-time library assistants and an information officer. They work in a specialist information service associated with a museum. Sam has never worked as a team leader before and her main concerns are that she is younger than her colleagues and has little experience of working in the museum sector as her previous experience was as a school librarian.

Case 1.2   Information skills team leader in an academic library

Jane has taken over responsibility for leading a team of six information skills specialists in an academic library. She is confident that she can do the job as she has just moved into her new role from a similar role elsewhere. Her main concern is that one of the team members made an unsuccessful application for the job. She is not looking forward to meeting this person for the first time.

Case 1.3 Leading a team of school librarians

David has been asked to lead a project team involving school librarians from secondary schools in the region. He is quite excited but also worried about his new role. How will he manage to lead a team when he is not the line manager of team members?

Whichever situation you are in, you will find that there are tried and tested approaches to supervising and leading teams and the purpose of this book is to provide appropriate guidance. Taking up the role of supervisor or team leader is exciting although it may be a little daunting at times. In order to develop your knowledge and skills in this area it is worthwhile understanding your role and responsibilities, the context in which you work, and also the strategic planning process. These are outlined in the following sections.

Understanding the role and the responsibilities

The process of understanding your role and responsibilities starts when you first apply for the job of supervisor or team leader. The job description will provide an outline of your roles and responsibilities. It is important to read this and to think about the following:

- Your team. Who is in the team and what are their roles and responsibilities?
- The work. What work is the responsibility of you and your team?
- Resources. What resources are your responsibility – buildings, information resources, ICT resources, intellectual property, finances?
- How do you fit into the ILS and organization?
- Who is your line manager? How does your work fit into their brief?

Thinking about these questions will help you to perform well at interview and also start to understand your new role. The example job advertisement in Figure 1.1 provides a good overview of a post of library supervisor but much more information is required for you to assess the job, e.g. if given the opportunity it may be useful to ask questions of the ILS managers or senior staff such as:

- What are the challenges involved in this role?
- What are the main strengths and weaknesses of the team?
- What are the future plans for the library and the team?

Activity: Your job role

How well do you know and understand your job role? Do you understand how your organization and ILS define your job? How do you link in with other parts of the ILS and organization? How do your expectations of your role match those of your line manager? If you are not clear about your job role then it is worthwhile spending some time finding out about it and thinking about how you and your role fit into the wider picture in the ILS and organization. A good starting point is likely to be your job description, organizational documents such as a structure diagram, and your manager.

The context of library and information work

The team leader or supervisor in the 21st century is likely to experience greater pressures, expectations and workloads than in the previous century as a result of

---

The Anytown Public Library Service is looking for an energetic and motivated library supervisor to manage the Small Road and Parkside Branch Libraries. You will lead and manage teams of library assistants to provide a high-quality customer service. Our libraries serve the whole community and provide lending services, reference services (printed and online) and public access computers.
Your duties will include:

- efficient running of the branch libraries
- staff management
- staff training and development
- provision of lending, reference and ICT services
- performance management
- general administration
- health and safety
- liaison with relevant managers and teams within the service.

You will have:

- good communication, interpersonal and customer-care skills
- organizational and problem-solving abilities
- leadership and management skills
- ICT skills (Office, Windows, e-mail and internet skills)
- the ability to work within the community and network with appropriate individuals and organizations
- the ability to manage the branch libraries through a period of change
- a positive approach to the continuous improvement of the services
- a relevant library or information qualification and/or library work experience and/or education to degree level (or equivalent).

The work is physically demanding. You will be required to work some evenings and weekends, and other hours when the libraries are open. You are required to travel between the branch libraries and also the services in the town centre.

Figure 1.1 Example of an advertisement including brief job description and person specification

a number of drivers that are influencing change in the world of work. Drivers for change include the rapid development of information and communications technology (ICT), globalization, new legislation, changes in organizational working, the rise of a project culture, and finally change in lifestyles and expectations of both information workers and also their customers. This changing landscape of work provides new opportunities for team leaders and supervisors, such as expanding employment possibilities, new ideas and practices, job enlargement, opportunities for project work, opportunities for different ways of working such as teleworking and working in virtual teams, as well as new possibilities for career progression.

In these times of continuous change and new challenges, leadership within the profession becomes very important at every level, e.g. the international and national professional communities, directors and managers in a particular ILS, and team leaders and supervisors. There is a great need for vision, innovation, detailed planning, implementation of plans and then evaluation and review. At the heart of this strategic process are team leaders and supervisors who are working with their teams to operationalize the plans and deliver the services, resources and products. While the literature on leadership is often couched in terms of senior managers and directors all team leaders and supervisors need to offer their information workers leadership within the framework of their ILS vision and strategic plan.

Team leaders and supervisors need to be able to manage the detail of the operations and this involves managing

- the people who do the work
- the actual work
- the material resources
- the working environment
- information and communications.

It may also involve managing external relations and finance.

Activity: Team leader and supervisor audit

You may use the personal inventory presented in Figure 1.2 as a way of considering your current knowledge and skills as a team leader and supervisor. You may use the results to identify which chapters of this book are particularly relevant to your needs and this may provide a starting point for your development process.

Team leader and supervisor audit

The purpose of this inventory is to help you reflect on your current skills as a supervisor or team leader. Please rate yourself as honestly as possible. Use your responses to identify areas for development. You may wish to discuss your scores with your manager or mentor.

	Please rate yourself on a score of 0 = absent 10 = high
Where are you now – knowledge?	
What is your knowledge of the organization? What is your knowledge of what the organization does? What is your knowledge of where the organization is going? What is your knowledge of the organization's vision, mission and strategic plan? What is your knowledge of the culture of the organization? What is your knowledge of the structure of the organization? What is your knowledge of the people in the organization?	
What is your knowledge of ILS practice? What is your knowledge of ILS customers? What is your knowledge of ILS services? What is your knowledge of ILS operations?	
What is your knowledge of management functions? What is your knowledge of people management? What is your knowledge of operations management?	
What is your knowledge of project management? What is your knowledge of change management? What is your knowledge of self-management?	
What is your knowledge of legal aspects? What is your knowledge of health and safety at work? What is your knowledge of intellectual property? What is your knowledge of legal aspects of human resource management?	
Where are you now – skills?	
How well developed are your communication skills? How well developed are your written communication skills? How well developed are your verbal communication skills? How well developed are your presentation skills? How well developed are your meeting skills? How well developed are your skills in dealing with challenging situations?	

Figure 1.2 Team leader and supervisor audit (continued on next page)

How well developed are your skills in managing people? How well developed are your skills in managing teams? How well developed are your skills in managing conflict? How well developed are your skills in managing workload? How well developed are your skills in managing personnel issues?	
How well developed are your skills in managing operations? How well developed are your skills in planning, e.g. workloads, project work? How well developed are your skills in managing staffing? How well developed are your skills in managing services? How well developed are your skills in managing buildings?	
How well developed are your skills in managing projects? How well developed are your skills in planning projects? How well developed are your skills in monitoring and controlling projects? How well developed are your skills in using project management tools and techniques such as Gantt charts and PERT diagrams?	
How well developed are your personal skills? How well developed are your skills in managing change? How well developed are your skills in managing your self? How well developed are your skills in managing your emotions? How well developed are your skills in managing time? How well developed are your skills in gaining support, e.g. through coaching and mentoring?	
Where are you now – attitudes?	
What does work mean to you? How important is work to you? What do you want to achieve? What type of work do you enjoy? How much change do you enjoy?	
Where do you want to be in terms of your career development? What type of work do you want to be involved in? What level of responsibility are you aiming for? Do you need to gain more qualifications to meet your goals? What type of work/life balance do you want to achieve now? What type of work/life balance do you want to achieve in the future?	

Figure 1.2 Team leader and supervisor audit (*continued from previous page*)

Background to approaches to management

To be an effective team leader or supervisor it is important to understand the different ways in which the organization and ILS work. In particular, it is important to understand the strategic thinking and planning processes that occur in all organizations either informally or through a formal strategic planning process. The reason for understanding the strategic planning process is that as a team leader you are likely to be asked to put parts of the strategic plan into operation, i.e. to make things happen. If you understand the strategic planning process then it will help you to understand the direction in which your organization and ILS is moving and also your role within this development process. This will help you to lead and motivate your team. The remainder of this chapter describes the strategic planning process that commonly takes place within organizations and ILS.

What is strategy? One useful definition of strategy is as follows:

> Strategy means control. It is the direction and scope of an organisation over the long term, ideally which matches its resources to its changing environment, and in particular its markets, customers or clients so as to meet stakeholder expectations.
>
> Johnson and Scholes (1999)

Organizations go through a regular strategic planning process and this often takes place on an annual basis. The strategic planning process is led by senior managers and may involve a consultative process. It is concerned with the long-term direction of the organization and ILS. In contrast, operational planning processes are directed by middle managers and are more concerned with short-term plans and the detailed planning of the day-to-day operations. Operational planning follows the organization's strategic plan. As a team leader or supervisor you are likely to be involved in following the strategic plan through operational planning and implementation. This means that it is important for you to read and understand the organization's and ILS's strategic plans.

The purpose of the strategic planning process is to identify where the organization and/or ILS is going and to plan how it will get there. The strategic planning process involves the following cycle: analysis, developing a strategy, implementation and management of change, and finally evaluation (see Figure 1.3). The process then starts again. Each of these stages is described in outline below.

Analysis

The purpose of the analysis stage is to gather information and this will be used as the basis for developing the strategic plan. This involves identifying factors in the external environment that will affect the organization and/or ILS such as politics, economics, society and technology. These are commonly called PEST factors. This analysis also involves analysing the particular sector that the organization and/or ILS is located in, e.g. health sector, higher education sector, financial services sector, and

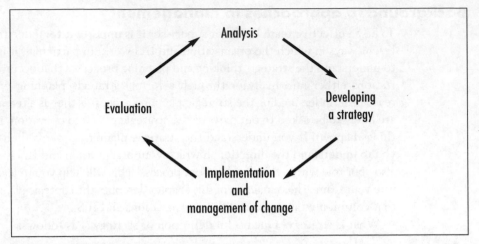

Figure 1.3 The strategic planning process

identifying relevant factors. In addition, the analysis stage also involves gathering information from inside the organization and/or ILS. It is customary to carry out a SWOT analysis to identify the strengths, weaknesses, opportunities and threats faced by the organization and ILS. The analysis stage may also involve identifying critical success factors, key assumptions and limiting factors.

Developing a strategy

This part of the process involves defining the overall thrust of the strategic plan by thinking through and identifying the following:

- *Vision*. Where do we want to be?
- *Values*. What is important to us?
- *Mission*. What is our purpose?
- *Major directions*
  — What major directions will we need to take to fulfil our vision?
  — What do we need to do to fulfil mission?
- *Critical success factors*
  — How will we know when we have achieved our mission?
  — What performance indicators will demonstrate our success?
- *Key assumptions*. What assumptions underpin this strategic thinking?
- *Limiting factors*. What are the limiting factors that will affect our progress?

The next stage of the strategic planning process involves producing detailed plans that outline the following:

- *Goals*. What is the overall aim or purpose?
- *Actions*. What are the steps required to achieve the goal(s)?
  — Production of action plans that outline specific tasks and activities that need to be carried out; these will identify who, what, where, when, and how the actions will be carried out
  — Production of relevant budgets and other resourcing statements.
- *Implementation*
  — Who will be responsible for implementing the plan?
  — How will it be monitored and controlled?
  — How will the action plans be monitored and controlled?
  — What reporting and feedback mechanisms will exist?
- *Management of change*
  — How will the people side of the change be managed?
  — How will the communications process be managed?
- *Review and evaluate*
  — How will the strategic planning and implementation process be reviewed and evaluated?
  — What review and feedback mechanisms will exist?

Implementation

This involves putting the action plans into practice and managing this process. This is likely to involve managing the action plan, managing and maintaining communications within the team and with other managers, identifying and resolving problems and unexpected events. It will involve organizing meetings to monitor and evaluate progress, and deciding on any changes that need to be made to the plans. It also involves ensuring that there is an appropriate working environment, and that health and safety arrangements are in place. It is at this stage that team leaders are likely to become heavily involved in the strategic process, as it is here that the action plans are put into practice within the ILS.

Management of change

The management of change process involves dealing with the people side of change and supporting them through the change process. For major changes this may involve changing the staffing structure, perhaps employing new staff, as well as training and development. Again, team leaders are likely to be very involved in this change process, as they will need to lead and manage their teams. This topic is covered in some depth in Chapter 3.

Evaluation

This part of the strategy process involves evaluating the effectiveness of the strategic plan and also the way in which the plan was implemented. At a very simple level it means deciding if the strategic plan produced an appropriate direction for the organization and how efficient and effective was the process of achieving the goals set in the plan. The evaluation stage may involve evaluating the overall strategic process, the use of different management tools, the effectiveness and the efficiency of the strategy, and also the impact, e.g. on customers, information workers, and other stakeholders. It is common practice for ILS to establish an evaluation team that will involve a wide range of staff from the service. Team leaders may be members of this team or may lead the team. In addition, they may be asked to contribute to the evaluation process.

How does senior management approach strategic change? There are two distinct approaches to implementing strategic change: the planning school and the incremental school. Leaders and managers who follow the planning school like to control the process, e.g. by producing a comprehensive hierarchy of checklists and techniques. This involves developing a planning by numbers culture with formal feedback routes. One of the disadvantages of this approach is that it may smother flexibility, imagination and risk-taking, and new opportunities that present themselves during the change process may be ignored. The other approach is called logical incrementalism and this involves managers having a clear vision and being flexible en route to their destination. Change takes place incrementally and takes into account people issues and political considerations. In some ways this approach to change involves senior managers, managers, team leaders and supervisors, and workers at the front line feeling their way to a known goal and learning and developing en route.

Activity: The strategic planning process

How well do you know and understand the strategic planning process in your organization? If you do not know and understand this process then it is worthwhile spending some time finding out about it, understanding the process and its implications for you and your team. A good starting point is likely to be organizational documents, e.g. strategic plan, and your own manager.

Summary

This chapter sets the context for leading and supervising teams in information and library services in the 21st century. The chapter provides an overview of the demands on team leaders and the knowledge and skills that are required to lead teams in a challenging work environment. Teamwork takes place within the context of an information and library service, and also an organization. This means that it is important for the team leader or supervisor to understand the organizational context including the strategic planning process. This enables you to understand the relationships between your work and that of the information and library service, and organization.

Reference

Johnson, G. and Scholes, K. (1999) *Exploring Corporate Strategy*, 5th edn, London, Prentice Hall.

2 Leading and managing the team

Introduction

The aim of this chapter is to provide an overview of different approaches to managing and leading teams. The main part of this chapter is concerned with providing a structured approach to managing the whole team. This is based around a series of questions relevant to both new and experienced team leaders. This is followed by a section that considers some theoretical models about team development and team roles. The final sections in this chapter consider the qualities of effective team leadership and also the 'seven deadly sins', or the ways in which teams are demotivated and destroyed.

Managing and leading teams

Leading, managing and supervising a team involves working with people to achieve the ILS objectives. The distinctions and differences between supervision, management and leadership are not explored in this chapter in any depth as the debate quickly moves into rather abstract territory. *Chambers Dictionary* provides the following definitions:

Leader 'A person who leads or goes first'
Manager 'A person who organizes other people's activities'
Supervisor 'A person who supervises. . . . To oversee, manage or direct operations.'

The work of a team leader or supervisor involves elements of leadership, management and supervision. Leadership takes place at a number of different levels: whole organization, e.g. chief executive officer, director, principal; individual departments, e.g. departmental manager or director; and teams, e.g. team leader, supervisor or senior library assistant. Leadership involves a mixture of personal qualities, such as the ability to inspire and motivate people, as well as skills in communicating and persuading others. Motivating the team is considered in some depth in Chapter 4. Good leaders inspire others to do their best at work and to strive to improve their performance and that of the organization. Effective leaders are confident, honest and have clear expectations of the team as a whole and also individuals. In addition, they will acknowledge problems and weaknesses, and not flinch from tackling awkward situations or problems. Finally, effective leaders are responsive to individual and team needs and concerns.

Roberts and Rowley (2004) identify the manager's role using a five-point task list. This is presented in Table 2.1 where it is compared with the role of the supervisor. It is worth noting that not all team leaders will be involved in the planning process for the ILS as a whole though they will be involved in implementing the organizational plans with their team. The main role of a supervisor is to ensure that the team works together to achieve the goals set by the organization. This involves making sure that there is an appropriate work environment; that the team provides the necessary services, systems and products to the required standards; that the team members are motivated and work together; and that individuals have the necessary training to do their work. In addition, the supervisor will play a key role as the co-ordinator of two-way communications between more senior staff and their team.

Table 2.1 The manager's and supervisor's roles

Broad task	Manager's role	Supervisor's role
Planning	Mission, strategic planning, objective setting	Planning the work of the team; objective-setting within the context of the organizational objectives
Organizing	Organizing work, decision-making, problem-solving	Organizing work, decision-making, problem-solving
Leading	Direction, motivation	Direction, motivation
Controlling	Discipline, performance review, monitoring	Discipline, performance review, monitoring
Achieving	Results	Results

Management textbooks often talk about leaders and managers using words such as authority, responsibility and accountability, and it is worthwhile considering the meaning of these words as they help to clarify the work of team leaders. Team leaders are given 'authority' or the right to make decisions and implement actions by their manager or director. Individual team leaders will have the authority to carry out certain tasks, e.g. establish staff rotas, organize the day-to-day work of the team. As a new team leader, it is sensible to identify the boundaries of your authority. The word 'responsibility' means that the team leader is expected to be responsive and to take appropriate action. For example, the team leader may be responsible for ensuring that a help desk is staffed from 9 a.m. to 9 p.m. This means that they will be expected to organize their team so that the desk is staffed; they are also expected to deal with events such as staff sickness and to ensure that they have contingency plans in place. Finally, team leaders are expected to be 'accountable' or answerable to their senior manager or director for their actions. This means taking praise for success in the workplace and also accepting responsibility if there are problems. The combination of authority, responsibility and accountability help to ensure that the team leader carries out the ILS's work and that decisions made by the senior management team are put into action.

In some organizations and ILS the levels of authority, responsibility and accountability of individual team leaders and supervisors are clearly laid out, e.g. in job specifications and person descriptions. In other organizations and, in particular, during times of change these boundaries may change or become blurred. The development of new ways of working, e.g. in multi-professional teams and collaborative teams, and virtual teams and organizations, means that team leaders may find themselves working in uncharted territories. This can be unsettling and also challenging, and it is perhaps best handled through an iterative process of discussion and reflection both within the team and also with the team leader's line manager and mentor. This situation is illustrated in Case study 7.2.

Team leaders and supervisors who are taking on a new role or who want to review their current practice will find it helpful to think about and reflect on their current situation. The following questions are useful in helping to start to review and reflect on your team and teamwork, and each question is explored in the following paragraphs:

- Do you know where you are going?
- Have team members the appropriate knowledge, skills and attitudes?
- Have you got the right type of working environment?
- Have you got a team that works together?
- Have you got the right kind of team leadership?
- Have you got appropriate support?

Do you know where you are going?

Where are you going? Successful supervisors and managers are those people who have an overview of their team and the ILS. They have an understanding of the vision, mission and goals of the ILS and know the outcomes their team is working towards. Knowing and understanding the ILS and team goals is vital as this helps you to manage and lead the team in the appropriate direction. You may find the following series of questions helpful to work through with your colleagues as a means of clarifying their direction:

- Why are we here?
- What are our organizational vision, mission, goal(s) and outcomes?
- What are our ILS vision, mission, goal(s) and outcomes?
- What are our team vision, mission, goal(s) and outcomes?
- What do people expect from us?
- What are the director's expectations?
- What are the senior managers' expectations?
- What are the customers' expectations?
- What are the other stakeholders' expectations?
- What do we expect of ourselves?

- What are the team leader's expectations?
- What are the team members' expectations?

Have team members the appropriate knowledge, skills and attitudes?

A key factor in successful team working is to ensure that individual team members have the appropriate skills, knowledge and attitudes for their work. As a team leader you need to ensure that you know the strengths of your team members and also identify areas for development. Chapter 8 covers the induction of new staff. Chapter 9 explores training and development and focuses on identifying individual and team training needs and different approaches to developing staff including e-learning, coaching and learning from reflection. Chapter 10 considers personal and professional development for team leaders and supervisors.

Have you got the right type of working environment?

It is important for team leaders to consider both the physical environment and also the organization of the work within this environment. The organization of the physical environment is important, as staff need to feel comfortable at work. It is sometimes helpful to review the layout and organization of the office and to identify areas of improvement. This is a task that is best carried out as a team activity because it gives people the opportunity to have an input into the organization of their working environment. This is illustrated in Case study 2.1. The topic of organizing the work environment is also considered in Chapter 5.

Case study 2.1   The office move

A university in the north of England was reorganizing its information services and developing a central information skills training team. The team of four were moved into a newly refurbished office close to the main enquiry desks. The team members had never shared an office before and their new team leader suggested that they visited the new office prior to their move and thought about how they wanted to organize the office. The university estates department provided the team leader with a copy of the room layout and she produced a series of cardboard cut-outs to represent the office furniture. The whole team spent part of their next team meeting playing with different layouts and, after much discussion, decided on a layout that catered for individual preferences. During the process, the new team began to get to know each other's likes and dislikes, and their feedback to their new team leader was that it had been a useful activity, not only as they were happy with the proposed layout but also because they felt they were beginning to bond as a new team. After six months in their new office they reviewed the layout and made some minor adjustments.

Have you got a team that works together?

Building the team is an ongoing process due to the almost constant change faced by ILS. Teams rarely stay the same due to resignations and new appointments, as well as organizational changes, e.g. mergers of departments or units. In addition, the work of the team may change as a result of the department or organization changing its direction resulting in new services, changes to existing services, and new customers or stakeholders. Nowadays there is a rise in collaborative working and teams may be established with staff working within the same or different ILS or across different ILS sectors, e.g. special ILS and public-sector ILS. In addition, teamwork may involve staff working within the same or different geographical locations, individuals teleworking, and also virtual teams who rarely or even never have face-to-face meetings. These types of teams are considered in more depth in Chapter 7. Teams that experience little change also require team building as a means of preventing stagnation and drift.

There are a number of different approaches to team building and it is perhaps worth highlighting that teams are not developed by one-off team-building events run by an external facilitator. Although this type of event is helpful in terms of introducing new ideas and perhaps unblocking bad habits, team building requires ongoing work led by the team leader. Peter Honey (1991) has identified positive behaviours that contribute to effective team work. See Table 2.2. This is a helpful list as the team leader may use it to identify and introduce strategies for developing the required behaviours. Common strategies include specific skills training, team development workshops, team appraisal processes, individual appraisal processes, role modelling of required behaviours, and rewarding wanted behaviours. Team development is considered later in this chapter and also in Chapter 4.

Table 2.2 Behaviours and teamwork

Wanted behaviour	Unwanted behaviour
Asking questions	Acquiescing
Suggesting ideas	Rubbishing ideas
Exploring alternatives	Going for expedient, quick fixes
Taking risks/experimenting	Being over-cautious or reckless
Being open about the way it is	Telling people what they want to hear; filtering news
Converting mistakes into learning	Repeating the same mistakes
Reflecting and reviewing	Rushing around keeping active
Talking about learning	Talking about anecdotes (i.e. what happened, not what was learnt)
Taking responsibility for self	Not taking responsibility; passing the buck
Admitting inadequacies and mistakes	Justifying actions; blaming others

Have you got the right kind of team leadership?

Management and leadership styles arise from the interplay between organizational culture and an individual team leader's personality, knowledge, skills and attitudes, and their experience. There are five main management styles: authoritative, participative, authoritarian, individualistic, laissez faire and chaotic (Mullins, 2006). These different styles are summarized in Table 2.3: each style is described in terms of how the manager makes decisions, the impact on team working, and also an example phrase that illustrates this style of management.

Table 2.3   Different management styles

Style	Decision-making	Impact on team	Typical comment from the team leader
Authoritative	The manager makes decisions that are within their power. They make it clear that their decisions can be questioned and discussed.	The manager tells team members what is expected of them. They provide guidance on what should be done and direct team members to follow standard rules and regulations.	'Do what I suggest.'
Participative	The decisions are made on the basis of consultation with the team. The manager shares decision-making authority with the team.	The manager and the team decide together how the team will work together. Much time may be spent in teams making decisions. The whole team is likely to own the decisions.	'Let us do it together.'
Authoritarian	The manager makes the decision and expects everyone to obey it without question. The manager exercises tight control over the team.	This style is usually characterized by communications from the manager downward to the team and not vice versa.	'Do what I say.'
Individualistic	The manager makes decisions that are not within their power, e.g. as a result of a management vacuum, or because they want to usurp or deny another person's legitimate authority.	This style is characterized by crises and feuds. The boundaries of the team are uncertain and there may be a sense of changing goal posts as the manager changes their mind or is asked to follow organizational working practices.	No one is making this decision, so I'll make it.'
Laissez-faire	This type of manager doesn't make decisions.	The team is often uncertain about what to do. Work may build up as decisions are not made. Individuals may take over and usurp the team leader's position and then feel resentful.	'If I ignore it then it will go away.'
Chaotic	There is no consistent style. The manager may shift between different styles, e.g. authoritarian and individualistic.	Chaos.	A mixture of: 'Do as I order'; 'Do it between us'; 'Do as I request'; 'You can do it well'; 'Let us discuss it all'; and 'Let's all be friends together.'

Authoritative and participative styles are generally very effective and good team leaders know when it is best to make a decision by themselves and when it is best to consult their team. They are comfortable making decisions themselves and know that it is best not to waste people's time by consulting unnecessarily or calling meetings to consult when they have already made their mind up about something. The other types of management styles, i.e. authoritarian, laissez-faire, individualistic and chaotic, are less effective and tend to leave a trail of destruction!

Have you got appropriate support?

Leading and managing a team can be a challenging job and, if you and your team are going through difficult experiences, it can be exhausting too. It is important that all team leaders identify and make use of appropriate support. This is likely to involve developing and nurturing constructive relationships with your manager, with other team leaders within your organization, with staff in departments such as the IT department and human resources department, as well as with a personal mentor. This topic is covered in more depth in Chapter 10.

Team development process

The next sections consider two important theoretical approaches to thinking about teams: the team development cycle; and team roles. Research into teams suggests that they go through a development cycle. This was originally described by Tuckman and Jenson (1977) as involving the following stages:

- forming
- storming
- norming
- performing
- adjourning or mourning.

This framework is useful as it offers ideas about how teams grow and develop, and it provides guidance on the ways in which a team leader can facilitate the team at any particular phase of its life history. However, the team development process is perhaps more complex than indicated in this model, e.g. a team may become stuck at a particular stage and teams that experience a rapid change-over of staff may never get beyond the forming process. The model suggests that team development is a linear process and that teams move from one phase on to the next phase. However, the team may experience a more complex life cycle, e.g. a well developed team may experience a process of forming as a new member arrives into the team but this quickly moves into performing as the team engages in its normal work activities with the new member being accepted and accepting the teams norms.

Knowing where a team is in the development process is very useful because it provides us with information about how people are likely to behave and also activities or processes that help the team move forward. Guidance on the ways in which a team leader may influence the team development process is given in Table 2.4.

Table 2.4 Stages in the life of a team

Stages	Typical team features	Typical attitudes towards the task, activity or project process	Team leader's interventions
Forming	The first stage. Individuals may feel anxious, uncertain or defensive. They may feel confident, enthusiastic and anxious to get started. This stage is frequently marked by individuals asking themselves the following questions: Have I made the right decision? Will I be liked? What will the others be like? In this stage, people begin to get to know each other; they may rush into 1:1 relationships or cliques. This stage is sometimes called the 'honeymoon period'.	What is the task? Team members seek the answers to that basic question, together with knowledge of the rules and methods to be employed. They may be concerned about the reliability of other members and their ability 'to deliver the goods'.	Provide direction; explain and clarify what is required within the team; enable team members to get to know each other.
Storming	At this stage conflicts between team members may become apparent as individuals want to make 'their mark' on the team. The limits of behaviour may be tested. Some team members may be rebellious either by action or inaction. They may challenge their manager or supervisor's authority. suggestions for activities may be challenged or rejected. There may be complaints about the project, team members, other teams or the team leader.	The value and feasibility of the task is questioned. People react emotionally against its demands.	Clarify boundaries; resolve tensions; defuse tensions and emotions.
Norming	In this stage, people begin to settle down and get on with the task. The unwritten rules or 'norms' or the team develop. Conflict is replaced by co-operation and team members start to talk about 'us; and 'we'. Cliques no longer exist and the team is comfortable about working in different sub-teams. There is a sense of 'team spirit' and humour will be present during project meetings. Mutual support develops.	Co-operation on the task begins; plans are made and work standards are laid down. Communication of views and feelings develops.	Support and enable the development of required norms and behaviours.

(continued on next page)

Table 2.4 (*Continued from previous page*)

Stages	Typical team features	Typical attitudes towards the task, activity or project process	Team leader's interventions
Performing	There is a high level of trust within the team. Individuals accept each other and their strengths and weaknesses. There is a strong commitment to achieving the team goals. Few teams reach this stage and if they do then the team is able to take control of itself. The team leader may feel redundant and may find it difficult to 'let go' of the team.	Constructive work on the task surges ahead; progress is experienced as more of the team's energy is applied to being effective in the area of the common task.	Stand back and enable them to perform; support team members and the team; praise their efforts.
Adjourning or mourning	The final stage in the life of a team. This may start a few weeks before the team formally ends. Team members will need time to celebrate their success, say their goodbyes and remember the high and low spots of their project experience.	It is marked by exchanges of addresses and phone numbers, arrangements for a celebration such as a meal out or another ritual mourning process.	Facilitate the ritual of ending the life of the team; help the team to remember its 'highs and lows'; celebrate the life and successes of the team and its members.

Initial meeting with the team

The initial team meeting is important as it is an opportunity for you to start the team forming process. If you are a new team leader then it is likely that you will meet your team members individually before you lead the first team meeting. The initial whole-group meeting is extremely important as it sets the tone for the future working of the team. It is really important that this meeting is organized in such a way that team members feel welcomed and that the future teamwork experience is going to be a positive one. Factors that can help oil the process include choosing a time when everyone can attend the meeting and that is scheduled to miss peak demands on the service; refreshments on arrival help too.

The agenda of this meeting is likely to include the following:

1 introductions
2 expectations – from team members and team leader
3 individual and team needs and contributions
4 areas of concern
5 team ground rules
6 discussion of intended team process including communication and reporting process
7 other questions and answers
8 outline action plan.

This initial meeting is all about getting to know each other and to begin thinking about how you can work together. In many ways the arrival of a new team leader offers a great opportunity to review the work of the team and to move forward. The meeting is also about identifying and agreeing working practices. A useful way of establishing team member and leader or manager responsibilities is to ask the meeting to split into sub-teams and to identify the responsibilities of team members and the team leader or manager. These can be shared and written up on a flipchart. The final list can then be used as an informal contract for the team. The team leader may find it useful to keep this flipchart paper because if people don't fulfil their responsibilities this activity can be revisited. An example of a list is given in Table 2.5.

Table 2.5 Supervisor and team responsibilities

Team members' responsibilities	Team supervisor's responsibilities
Carry out all individual duties to a high quality.	Be available to staff.
Provide cover for others both on the rota and also at periods of high demand.	Liaise with other departments, supervisors and managers.
Support team members and supervisor.	Keep the team informed of developments within the ILS.
Inform team of current or potential problems.	Allocate work and prioritize when the workload is too high.
Provide or suggest potential solutions to problems.	Deal with difficult or awkward situations.
Manage own time and relieve colleagues at service points five minutes before switch-over time.	Help staff if they are having difficulties with a particular piece of work.
Enter relevant information in desk diary.	Listen to staff and their concerns, and support and encourage staff.
Keep workplace tidy.	Give positive feedback and support to the team.
Support their team supervisor.	Enable staff to develop and improve their performance at work.

It is worthwhile using some time at the first meeting to let people air any concerns, fears or unhappiness about working in the team. One way of managing this process is to ask the team to work in groups of three or four and to identify their hopes and fears for their involvement in the team. They can then give feedback to the whole team. In the feedback process it is important to ask for the 'fears' first as this will raise any negative issues. Once these have been dealt with then move on to the hopes. Managing the process in this way will mean that you end up on a positive note. If necessary set a time limit on the feedback process or limit each team to two fears and two hopes. This helps to prevent the whole process being swamped by potential negativity. At this stage, it is worth mentioning that the majority of teams are made up of positive and constructive staff!

Case studies 2.2 and 2.3 illustrate some practical approaches to team development.

Case study 2.2 The new team

A collaborative project team was established as part of an externally funded project to establish an information skills portal. The project team included staffs from two universities and three further education colleges. The project team included the project manager, a library representative from each institution, a webmaster and a project administrator. At the first meeting the project manager suggested that the new team establish a set of ground rules for working together. After some discussions they came up with the following list:

- attend all meetings and be punctual
- communicate clearly and honestly
- communicate regularly, e.g. answer all e-mails within two working days
- let project team know when you are away on holiday
- exchange information – don't keep useful information to yourself
- identify problems (and come up with potential solutions)
- pull your weight and do a fair share of the work
- keep promises and meet agreed deadlines
- provide refreshments if the project team meets at your institution.

This list was then e-mailed to all members. The project was extremely successful and, in the evaluation, individual team members said that having an agreed set of ground rules from the beginning allayed some of their fears about being involved in the project.

Case study 2.3 Moving into uncharted territories

This case study illustrates how an information professional moved from an information department in the publishing industry to a new role in an e-commerce company where she was required to research and construct a hierarchy of products and services to be used on the company website. The following quotation illustrates some of the challenges involved in setting up a team in a new environment and learning how to work with other teams.

I've now been at BuyerWeb for a year and have no regrets about my decision. The change in culture was abrupt, but very pleasant. I found the relaxed, casual atmosphere among the twelve employees at the time a breath of fresh air after working at a large corporation for so many years. Within six weeks I had hired two other librarians, 'Content Developers,' to join the team. Our office was cramped — for example, for the first eight months I shared a cubicle with one of the other members of the team.

From the beginning, I was made to feel as if my department's efforts were key to making our business successful, but the first six months were very challenging for all of us. Prior to my arrival, content had been researched and created by the tech team. Since they had researched and created forms for several categories before I'd come on board, they had definite ideas about how the content (hierarchy and forms) should be developed and about standards to be used. In some cases we had different ideas. There was a lack of communication between our departments, which led to misunderstandings. Some of the problems stemmed from the lack of an initial orientation, which would have provided us with essential background information.

Our team was second-guessed on many of our decisions on content, standards, form layout, design, vocabulary, and user interface. We felt unappreciated for our skills and knowledge as librarians. The tech team felt as if we didn't value their input and experience. Finally, the Chief Technical Officer and I hashed out a plan for his team to meet with us weekly until we were fed all the information we needed to understand their insights and make informed decisions. Over the course of several months we laid the groundwork for a real team effort. We continue to nurture the communication between our departments, and by now have developed an excellent working relationship.

Leon (2000)

Activity: Team development process

Look at Table 2.4 and reflect on this framework with respect to your own team. Which stage do you think your team is at? What evidence have you used to make this judgement? How could you use this model to help develop your team? You may find it helpful to explore these ideas with your team, trusted colleagues or your manager.

Team roles

One traditional approach to exploring teamwork is to look at the different types of contributions or team roles that characterize individual behaviour within the team. There are a number of different theoretical models on team roles. The one developed by Meredith Belbin (1993) is presented here as it is readily understood, widely used and accepted, and it provides a useful diagnostic tool. According to Belbin, effective teams are those teams that are made up of a mixture of people who together represent the range of team roles given in Table 2.6. Less effective teams are likely to be those where some team roles are not naturally represented within the team. Further information is available at www.belbin.com/.

Table 2.6 Summary of Belbin team roles

Note: The language used in this table comes from Belbin's work.

Type	Typical features	Positive qualities	Allowable weaknesses
Company worker	Conservative, dutiful, predictable	Organizing ability, practical common sense, hard-working, self-discipline	Lack of flexibility, unresponsiveness to unproven ideas
Chair	Calm, self-confident, controlled	A capacity for treating and welcoming all potential contributions on their merits and without prejudice; a strong sense of objectives	No more than ordinary in terms of intellect or creative ability
Shaper	Highly strung, outgoing, dynamic	Drive and a readiness to challenge inertia, ineffectiveness, complacency or self-deception	Proneness to provocation, irritation and impatience
Plant	Individualistic, serious-minded, unorthodox	Genius, imagination, intellect, knowledge	Up in the clouds; inclined to disregard practical details or protocol
Resource investigator	Extroverted, enthusiastic, curious, communicative	A capacity for contacting people and exploring anything new; an ability to respond to challenge	Liable to lose interest once the initial fascination has passed
Monitor–evaluator	Sober, unemotional, prudent	Judgement, discretion, hard-headedness	Lacks inspiration or the ability to motivate others
Team worker	Socially orientated, rather mild, sensitive	An ability to respond to people and to situations, and to promote team spirit	Indecisiveness at moments of crisis
Completer–finisher	Painstaking, orderly, conscientious, anxious	A capacity for follow-through; perfectionism	A tendency to worry about small things; a reluctance to 'let go'

Belbin's model is commonly used on team-building programmes and events as it provides a common language that individuals may use to explore their team roles. In addition, it is useful in helping to identify any gaps within the team. However, there are dangers in using this type of model as it may be used to stereotype and label individuals. In reality, people are sophisticated and adept at moving into different roles as and when required in different situations.

Team leaders and the seven deadly sins

How can this theory be turned into action? This section presents the findings, including quotations, from a survey of 343 library staff members who responded to an online survey on their managers' qualities and effectiveness (Gordon, 2004). The findings from this survey are useful as they are a clear indication from grass-roots level of what information and library staff want from their supervisors and managers, and also what they don't want. These findings are summarized in Table 2.7 and presented below with quotations from the original survey.

Table 2.7   Effective team leaders (and also the seven deadly sins)

Seven strategies for effective team leaders	Seven deadly sins
Encouraging growth	Micromanagement
Providing autonomy	Lack of communication
Looking out for staff	Fostering divisiveness
Respecting everyone's contribution	Abusiveness
Leading by example	Failure to listen
Communicating and listening	Avoiding conflict
Providing leadership and vision	Taking credit for others' work

Micromanagement

In the survey, micromanagement was the employees' most common complaint and this occurs when team leaders don't trust their team members to carry out their work to the required standard. Micromanagers want to get involved in every detail of the work of the team and don't stand back and let their staff get on with their work. The effects of micromanagement are a demotivated team, time-wasting on checking and talking about inappropriate levels of detail and an overloaded team leader.

> She could not let go of any project and had to second-guess me every step of the way . . . She did not trust her employees to do anything but the most mundane tasks without her direct supervision.

Lack of communication

This occurs for a number of different reasons, e.g. the team leader may:

- assume that team members have the required information
- be unwilling to deliver bad news
- want to hoard information on the basis that 'information is power'
- not schedule in time for communicating with individuals and the team as a whole.

> The worst library manager I ever had was a very poor communicator . . . I often didn't have the information I needed to do my job well or at all. I often just couldn't understand her. I often wasn't sure what she expected of me.

Fostering divisiveness

This may occur in a number of different ways such as showing favouritism to one or more members of staff, playing departments or teams against one another, treating staff in different roles in different ways, e.g. the 'professional' and 'non-professional' staff divide. Team leaders who foster divisiveness and treat different people in different ways produce a team made up of competing and anxious individuals who find it hard to work together.

> The worst library manager I ever had did not respect my years of service and my capabilities because I did not have a master's degree. She did not include me in discussions, and . . . ostracized me from my Youth Services team.

Abusiveness

Some team leaders use sarcasm, put-downs and other bullying tactics. Although many organizations have anti-bullying policies and procedures this behaviour does still exist in the workplace in some organizations.

> This person routinely treated staff as if they were idiots, ignoring staff opinions and sometimes actually yelling at staff in front of others.

Failure to listen

This is a common problem as some team leaders do not listen to their staff and ignore their opinions and perspectives. This type of manager is very demotivating to work with and the end result of this behaviour is a loss of morale and team members not engaging with workplace activities or issues.

Avoiding conflict

If problems or difficult situations are avoided then they will fester and grow.

Avoiding conflict may involve not backing up a colleague, e.g. in front of a reader who wants the librarian to break standard procedures, or ignoring personal conflicts.

Avoided confrontation to the point of destruction of teamwork and morale, staff fell apart.

Taking credit for others' work

It is very annoying when someone takes credit for your idea, or, they turn down your idea and then a few days later present it as their own.

Before you even opened your mouth, her answer was 'no'. And then two days later this was 'her' idea and it was implemented.

Seven strategies for effective team leaders
Encouraging growth

Effective team leaders encourage growth and development of team members as this enables individuals to improve their performance and also develop their careers. Managers who don't encourage growth are likely to end up with a demotivated team who are unable to cope with the changing demands of the information and library service.

I am encouraged to think outside the box and am always given the benefit of her guidance when I need it, her advice when I want it, and her support when the best-laid plans go awry. I grow every day under her tutelage.

Providing autonomy

Autonomy is the opposite of micromanagement. Team leaders who enable their team to work autonomously show that they respect and trust their colleagues. This approach helps to develop and encourage professionalism. Individuals may make mistakes and will deal with them in a professional and honest manner. Providing autonomy enables individuals to develop their self-confidence and learn how to deal with a wide range of situations in an appropriate manner.

I most appreciate a manager who treats employees like adults – assumes that we're all professionals, and we will get the job done, although some of us have different styles.

Looking out for staff

Managers who look out for their team will defend them and support them when they are being challenged or under threat. This helps to develop a sense of loyalty in the team both to their leader and each other.

> He looked out for us as his number one priority. He always defended us and our workload/workflow with the administration.

Respecting everyone's contribution

Effective team leaders respect everyone's contribution and recognize that different team members contribute in different ways and at different levels. Respecting and remembering to acknowledge the contribution of different people is important because it helps to maintain morale and motivation. In addition, if team members see that everyone's contribution is respected then it helps to develop respect for each other.

> They should most definitely praise good work when they see it, as this helps to motivate the team. Lack of appreciation can be very demoralizing.

Leading by example

Leading by example is impressive and being able to take a hands-on approach when appropriate is one way in which team leaders can enhance their credibility and authority. The survey found that respondents were extremely negative about the 'Do as I say, not as I do' syndrome.

> Even though she was management, she still worked the desk right alongside us and helped out when staff was short. She was a great reference librarian and kept up her research skills.

Communicating and listening

It is impossible to overemphasize the importance of communicating and listening to staff. Team members who have a good understanding of the ILS and the decisions and reasoning behind the decisions made by senior managers within the ILS or parent organization are more likely to work with and accept changes. They will develop a good knowledge about and be able to discuss current issues and decisions. This means that they are more likely to input their own thoughts and ideas into consultation processes and also engage with the ILS's stakeholders in an informed manner.

> The best manager that I worked for allowed for open communication, even of difficult issues. She was open and honest and made herself available to employees to discuss whatever might come up in the workplace.

Providing leadership and vision

It is important that team leaders and managers are able to provide leadership and vision. This means knowing where the team is going and how this fits into the vision of the ILS and parent organization. It also means being able to articulate this vision in a meaningful and enthusiastic manner. Sometimes this involves translating the vision of the parent body into a concrete statement that is meaningful to the team.

The need for a leader with clear articulated goals is so vital. The ability to make the vision a reality and make staff excited to be a part of it.

Activity: Your own approach to leading and supervising your team

Look again at Table 2.7 and consider the strengths and weaknesses of the effective team leader. What are your strengths? Identify one weakness that you demonstrate and identify ways in which you could change this habit. You may find it helpful to discuss this activity with a colleague, your manager or mentor.

Summary

There is no magic formula for leading or managing teams. Effective team leaders often use authoritative and participative styles of leadership, and are flexible in their approach to leading the team. They invest time in building and developing their team, and they get to know and respect individual team members taking into account the diverse needs of individuals. Research into team leaders suggests that information and library staff want to be led by individuals who provide leadership and vision; encourage their growth and development; provide autonomy; communicate and listen; lead by example; respect everyone's contribution; and look out for and support their team within the ILS and organization.

References

Belbin, M. (1993) *Team Roles at Work*, London, Butterworth Heinemann.

Gordon, R. S. (2004) *Seven Deadly Sins (and Desirable Strategies) for Library Managers*, www.freepint.com/ (accessed 24 May 2006).

Honey, P. (1991) *Teams and Teamwork*, Aylesbury, Peter Honey Publications.

Leon, D. (2000) *Working for an Internet Start Up*, www.sla.org/content/shop/information/infoonline/2000/Aug00/edge.cfm (accessed 30 July 2006).

Mullins, L. (2006) *Management and Organisational Behaviour*, 7th edn, London, FT/Prentice Hall.

Roberts, S. and Rowley, J. (2004) *Managing Information Services*, London, Facet.

Tuckman, B. W. and Jenson, M. A. (1977) Stages of Small Group Development Revisited, *Group and Organization Studies*, **2**, 419–27.

3 Confident leadership and supervision

Introduction

The purpose of this chapter is to introduce a range of ideas that will help the new and developing team leader or supervisor to become confident in working with others. This chapter offers a number of different models that may be used by team leaders as a tool for reflection and personal development.

The chapter starts by considering some of the characteristics of confident team leaders. This is followed by the presentation of the assertiveness model which offers a useful framework for exploring, understanding and developing individual behaviour. The concept of emotional intelligence was developed in the USA in the 1990s and this model is presented here because it offers a pragmatic approach to exploring the emotional side of leading and working in teams. This chapter includes a section on problem solving and provides a framework for tackling problems in the workplace. This is supported by a long case that demonstrates the application of problem-solving techniques to the type of problem that commonly arises in libraries and information services. Finally, the issue of the management of change is outlined and developed through a framework that explores individual responses to change.

Confident leadership and supervision

Confident supervisors and team leaders are people who are able to lead their teams: they know where they are going; they have a range of strategies for getting there; and are able to handle the people issues that inevitably arise in a clear and honest manner. These leaders and supervisors may not always know the 'right answer' or the 'best approach' to carrying out a task but they have the confidence and leadership skills to work with their team and others to identify and put into place the most appropriate set of actions. While confident team leaders still experience the types of problems and situations common to many teams, e.g. personality clashes, problems with disaffected and demotivated staff and high workloads, they will be pro-active in bringing these issues out into the open and attempting to solve them. An analysis of the ways in which confident supervisors and team leaders work produces the following list of common characteristics.

Confident supervisors and team leaders:

- know what they want the team to achieve and have a clear sense of the team's goals and outcomes;
- articulate the goals and outcomes in a clear manner and without succumbing to 'management speak'; this often means that they need to translate the organizational goals-and outcomes into the language relevant for a particular team or department;
- are aware of their own feelings and are sensitive to others, and this will be reflected in their language, e.g. 'I'm not comfortable with this . . .' or 'I'm not sure how to deal with this issue. I'm going to discuss it with colleagues in the human resources department before I come back to you';
- respect themselves and others and this will be demonstrated by their having clear boundaries. For example, if they ask a member of staff to work an extra evening duty they will respect their colleague's right to turn down this request and not become involved in attempting to bully or blackmail them into doing an additional duty;
- are open about what they think and how they feel; they are able to present this in a non-threatening and non-manipulative manner. They will give others the opportunity to say how they think or feel within a safe and supportive culture;
- feel comfortable giving constructive feedback.

Different models of communication can be used to help articulate and explore the characteristics of confident supervisors and team leaders. I have selected two approaches based on their relevance and usefulness to practising team leaders and supervisors. These are the assertiveness model and the concept of emotional intelligence.

The assertiveness model

The assertiveness model was developed during the 1970s. It is still relevant today because it provides a clear framework for thinking about and developing our communication skills. Useful introductory guides to assertiveness include Back and Back (1999) and Dickson (2002). The assertiveness model suggests that different behaviours, such as assertive, aggressive and passive, have different effects on the people with whom we are communicating. The characteristics of these three behaviours are outlined in Table 3.1.

As a team leader or supervisor it is helpful to practise assertive behaviour. It is perhaps worth remembering the communication pie chart (see Figure 3.1) which shows that body language counts for 58% of the process, our tone of voice 35%; the actual words we use are only 7% of the whole process (O'Connor and Seymour, 1993).

Table 3.1   The assertiveness model

	Assertive	**Aggressive**	**Passive**
Body language	Open body language: relaxed, calm; good eye contact; standing square with feet on ground	May involve pointing or threatening gestures; tense; staring eyes; invasion of someone else's space	Closed body language: tense or 'switched off'; poor or no eye contact; looks small
Verbal language	Speaks clearly; uses 'I . . .' statements; makes clear and positive statements; uses clear, straightforward language	Shouts or is loud; uses words such as 'should' and 'must'; makes demands; makes threatening statements; uses rude, abusive language	Quiet; apologises; agrees with others; acquiesces

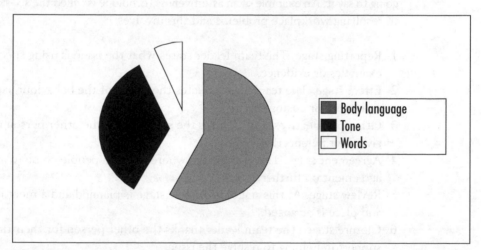

Figure 3.1   The communication pie chart

In terms of being an assertive team leader it is most important to think about your body language and work towards having an open posture with feet squarely upon the ground and making good-quality eye contact. If you feel as if your body language is not assertive and confident then think about practising assertive behaviour as much as possible. In addition, you may wish to attend a training event or workshop that will help you to become more assertive. Many professional associations and large employers regularly organize this type of event.

Activity: Assertiveness skills

Practise and develop your assertiveness skills. Examples of assertiveness activities include:

- Practise assertive body language in a range of situations, e.g. when shopping, in hotels, on the phone to marketing companies, in the workplace.
- Several times a day take time out (this will only take a few seconds each time) and check your body language. Do you have an open posture with feet squarely upon the ground? Are you making good-quality eye contact?

The assertiveness literature offers specific techniques for dealing with issues in the workplace. The basis of many of these techniques involves thinking about and planning how to tackle the issue, structuring the intervention in a logical manner, and then practising the technique, e.g. with a friend or trusted colleague. Once you have tackled the situation then you are advised to reflect on it and learn from what went well and what could be improved. This process helps you to go into challenging situations well prepared and clear about what you are going to say and how you are going to say it. An example of an assertiveness technique is called the six-stage process to resolving workplace problems and this involves:

1 Reporting stage. The team leader states what the issue is using specific examples or evidence.
2 Effect stage. The team leader relates the effect of the behaviour, e.g. on colleagues or customers.
3 Other perspectives stage. This is the stage where the other person is asked to give their perspective.
4 Agreement stage. This is the stage where the two people come to an agreement on further action.
5 Review stage. At this stage the review stage is planned and a meeting time and place is arranged.
6 Closure stage. The team leader thanks the other person for their time and support in helping to resolve the issue.

Case study 3.1 illustrates the use of the six-stage process in tackling the issue of poor timekeeping in the workplace.

Case study 3.1   Assertiveness in practice
Wen is a team leader for an information desk working within a legal library. She has four colleagues and one of them, Jan, is persistently late back from lunch. Wen decides to tackle this issue and asks Jan into her room. Wen uses the following assertive process to help structure her talk with Jan.

1 First she informs Jan that she has observed that she is often up to half an hour late back from lunch and gives specific dates and times (Reporting stage).
2 Next, she expresses her concerns about this behaviour. It makes it difficult to staff the help desk; it causes tension within the team; Jan is doing less work than her

colleagues; the law firm is regularly losing up to two hours of Jan's time each week (Effect stage).

3 Next, Wen asks Jan if she wants to say anything. Jan explains that she is hopeless with time but is willing to stay late to make up any lost time (Other perspective stage).

4 Next, Wen and Jan agree that in future Jan will set the alarm on her mobile phone ten minutes before her lunch break is over. She will work hard at getting back on time. If she is late then she will repay that time by working late (agreement stage).

5 Next, Wen suggests that they arrange to meet in a fortnight to review the situation (Review stage).

6 Finally, Wen thanks Jan for attending the meeting. She gives her general positive feedback about her work (Closure stage).

Throughout this process Wen ensured that her body language and verbal language were both assertive.

In some situations it is best to manage this type of discussion by using the six-stage process in a slightly different order and allowing the other person to give their perspective first. This can be particularly useful in challenging situations or when the other person is very emotional and needs to 'let off steam' before they can listen and discuss the issue. This means that the order of the process is:

1 Other perspectives stage
2 Reporting stage
3 Effect stage
4 Agreement stage
5 Review stage
6 Closure stage.

This is illustrated in Case study 3.2.

Case study 3.2   'Work has changed'

Mick has worked in the library for 25 years and is one of the longest-serving members of staff. His new team leader, David, has noticed that Mick appears to do less work than other team members, e.g. he spends less time on the help desk and his individual respons- ibilities appear to be minimal. In addition, Mick regularly takes long coffee and lunch breaks. A number of team members have complained directly about Mick or they have made comments about him within David's hearing. David talks with his manager, Joan, who confirms that the situation with Mick has drifted and has never been properly tackled.

David decides to tackle the issue. He asks Mick to come and see him to discuss his work within the team. First, David gives Mick a chance to have his say (Other perspective). Mick says that overall he is happy in his work but that at times he feels very pressurized. He doesn't like working on the help desk as he flounders with some of the

IT questions asked by the readers. Mick is happy with his individual responsibilities but says that the amount of cataloguing he does is now limited. He feels that he is the oldest person in the department and that some of the younger staff do not respect him or his professional knowledge. He enjoys his breaks and lunch as he meets up with two friends who have also very long service within the library and they can talk about 'the good old days'.

David then summarizes Mick's response and adds that it fits into his observations with respect to Mick's work on the help desk, individual workload and also the importance of his breaks to him. He outlines the problem with respect to long coffee and lunch breaks and gives specific examples to back up his comments (Reporting stage). He outlines the tensions that this causes within the team (Effect stage). David then responds by saying that he appreciates the wealth of knowledge and experience that Mick brings to the department. David says that he was aware of the drop in the cataloguing workload and asked Mick how he would feel about getting involved in a new project to document all the working procedures within the department. Mick's long-term experience would enable him to do this job particularly well and he could then become more involved in staff training. David then goes on to suggest that perhaps Mick would benefit from some training to help him to get to grips with the IT queries that he faces at the help desk. Mick readily agrees with this suggestion. Finally, David tackles the issue of timekeeping over breaks. He presents this by suggesting that time keeping is important (Mick agrees with this) and that more experienced colleagues need to set a good example to other colleagues by good timekeeping. Mick agrees and says that he will try to keep his breaks on time. He offers to work late if his breaks overrun in future (Agreement stage).

Overall, David is satisfied with the discussion. Mick appears to be in agreement, i.e. his body language matches his verbal agreements with David. David suggests that it would be a good idea if he summarizes their decisions in an e-mail and that they meet again in six weeks' time to discuss progress. Mick agrees with this course of action (Review stage). Finally, David closes the meeting by reiterating the value of Mick's contribution to the team and the wealth of knowledge and experience that Mick brings to the department. He thanks Mick for attending the meeting and working with him on a productive solution (Closure).

Another way of thinking about assertive behaviour is to consider what is going on 'in our heads' and our inner self-talk. This is illustrated in Figure 3.2 that shows that if you are in a particular situation then you are likely to experience inner self-

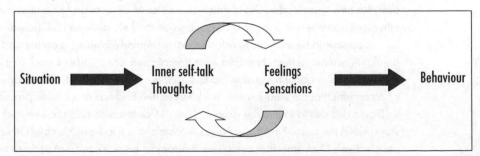

Figure 3.2 Impact of self-talk on behaviour

talk. Assertive behaviour is linked to how people feel about themselves and their particular situations.

If a team leader is working in a context where they do not feel very confident then a cycle (see Figure 3.3) leading to non-assertive behaviour (either passive or aggressive depending on the personality of the team leader and the situation) may take place.

When team leaders feel comfortable with themselves and confident in their abilities then the cycle illustrated in Figure 3.4 is likely to be taking place in the workplace situation and this results in assertive behaviour being maintained. Case study 3.3 shows how changing self-talk can help team leaders to feel confident about their work.

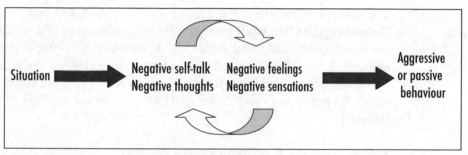

Figure 3.3 Non-assertive behaviour

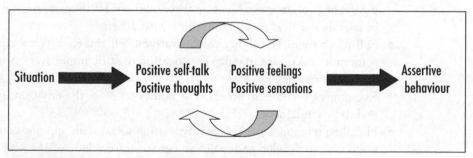

Figure 3.4 Assertive behaviour

Case study 3.3   Chairing meetings

George was the supervisor of the website team in a government office. He enjoyed his job but found chairing team meetings very difficult. He was convinced that staff thought he was a poor chair and that he waffled when talking about current issues. He tackled this issue in the following ways:

- He asked a trusted colleague to sit in on one of the meetings and give him feedback. This took place and the feedback was positive. The only suggestion for change was that George should encourage quieter team members to speak in the meeting.

- George reflected on his self-talk and realized that before and during meetings he said negative things to himself such as 'I can't do this as well as John' and 'I am sounding boring.' He decided to change his self-talk to 'I am good at running effective meetings' and he repeated this sentence to himself whenever he caught himself in negative self-talk.

It took several months and George had probably repeated the sentence 'I am good at running effective meetings' hundreds of times before he noticed that his negative self-talk diminished and he became more confident and assertive in chairing meetings.

Emotional intelligence

The concept of emotional intelligence was developed and promoted by Daniel Goleman in the USA. While there is some debate about the value of the concept of emotional intelligence, which involves traits such as social deftness, persistence and empathy, it does offer a practical approach to exploring and understanding emotions in the workplace. In addition, it offers an approach to personal and team development. According to Daniel Goleman (1995) emotional intelligence involves the following:

- Self-awareness. Knowing one's own emotions.
- Managing emotions. The ability to identify and manage one's own emotions, e.g. feelings of disapointment or anger, and not let them inappropriately impact on our lives and relationships with others.
- Self-motivation. The ability to motivate ourself and to recognize that it is sometimes necessary to delay gratification or stifle impulsiveness in order to achieve our goals.
- Recognizing emotion in others. The ability to 'read' the emotions of others and to be empathetic.
- Handling relationships. This involves using social skills and our emotional awareness to develop and maintain constructive relationships with others.

This concept of emotional intelligence is relevant to team leaders and supervisors and it offers a useful tool for reflection. This is demonstrated in Case study 3.4.

Case study 3.4   Emotional intelligence

Brigit was the team leader of the research team in a European company based in Paris. She supervised a team of three staff and they worked in a very busy department. Brigit generally had good relationships with her team but on several occasions individual members of staff had emotional outbursts. During the latest outburst, her colleague Sam called Brigit 'a cold fish'. Brigit was quite shaken by this outburst and talked with her friends about it that night over a meal. One of her friends suggested that perhaps Brigit had not read the emotions of the situation and had ignored signs of stress in her colleagues. This friend also mentioned the idea of 'emotional intelligence'. Brigit reflected on this comment and decided that there was probably some truth in it. She read up a little about emotional intelligence over the internet and decided to spend more time noticing the emotions of others. As a result, Brigit became more sensitive to the emotions of her colleagues. She learnt to ask about how others were feeling and take this into account in her relationships with others. One important point that she realized was that if she was under pressure then she tended to ignore the feelings of others and treat them like robots. She learnt that the more pressure there was at work then the more important it was to create a positive emotional atmosphere to enable the work to take place.

Activity: Emotional intelligence

The questionnaire presented in Figure 3.5 provides a process tool that you may like to use to identify and reflect on your emotional intelligence. Complete the questionnaire and reflect on your responses. You may find it helpful to discuss your responses with a trusted colleague or friend. In addition, you could use this questionnaire as part of a team-building activity.

This questionnaire is not a scientific measuring tool but a process tool that you may like to complete either working by yourself, with colleagues or friends, or with the team. The results may form the focus for reflection for personal development.

Aspects of emotional intelligence	Questions	Never	Rarely	Usually	Always
Self-awareness	1. I am normally aware of my feelings. 2. I am aware of subtle changes in my feelings. 3. I am normally aware of my body language and how it matches my feelings.				
Managing emotions	4. I don't let my feelings get in the way of my relationships at work. 5. If I am feeling emotional at work then I defer making important decisions. 6. If I am angry then I manage my emotions so that my actions or words are not destructive.				

Figure 3.5 Emotional intelligence process tool (*continued on next page*)

Aspects of emotional intelligence	Questions	Never	Rarely	Usually	Always
Self-motivation	7. I am self-motivated and willing to work towards my goals. 8. I am willing to work hard so that I can achieve my goals. 9. If I experience a setback then I can keep going and remain optimistic.				
Recognizing emotions in others	10. I am good at 'reading' the feelings of others. 11. I notice small changes in the emotions of others. 12. Colleagues tell me that I am empathetic and understand their feelings.				
Handling relationships	13. I can handle conflict and emotional upsets in the team. 14. I can sense and recognize the feelings in a group. 15. I can normally find the appropriate words to say to someone who is upset or angry.				
When you review your answers then it is your responses to the left of the page that are perhaps worth focusing on.					

Figure 3.5 Emotional intelligence process tool (*continued from previous page*)

Problem solving

Team leaders are often called upon to help solve problems and this section provides general guidance on problem solving. Many different types of problems arise in the workplace and they can be divided into recurrent and non-recurrent problems. These are illustrated in Table 3.2.

Problem-solving techniques are often used to tackle recurrent problems, e.g. the

Table 3.2 Recurrent and non-recurrent problems

Recurrent problems	Non-recurrent problems
Computer breakdowns	Supplier of library system goes out of business
Staff shortages	Threatening behaviour from a reader
Lift breakdown	Theft
Long queues at a service point	Bomb threat
Broken links on a website	Fire or flood

problem of long queues at a service point may be dealt with using a technique to identify a number of potential solutions including improved guiding, improved level of staffing, staff training, longer opening hours, provision of self-service machines. Problem solving is also used for some kinds of non-recurrent problems, e.g. tackling the situation of the supplier of the library computer system going out of business. Other types of non-recurrent problems, e.g. bomb threats or unacceptable behaviour from a reader, are more often dealt with through forward planning resulting in the development of appropriate policies and procedures. It is worth noting that the development of these policies and procedures is likely to involve an element of problem solving.

One of the major difficulties with solving problems is that too often individuals and teams rush into a solution without properly analysing the situation and a number of different solutions. A good starting point in problem solving is to consider a wide range of perspectives including:

1 The importance of the issue. Is the issue worthwhile resolving? At which level within the ILS does it need to be resolved, e.g. senior managers or team leaders and their teams? Do other people need to be involved, e.g. human resources department?
2 Is it a recurrent or non-recurrent issue? Recurrent issues can often take up a lot of staff time and although the problem in itself may not be important the consequences of its recurrence are important. Some non-recurrent issues are emergencies and it is best to have an emergency plan to enable you to deal with them.
3 Different stakeholder perspectives. Consider the problem from the perspectives of different stakeholders, e.g. customers, suppliers, ILS staff.
4 Identify ILS and organizational perspectives. Some problems are not worth solving because they are being tackled at the organizational level rather than the ILS level. In this instance, if the ILS goes ahead and identifies and implements a solution then it may not fit in with the organization's plans.
5 Identify long- and short-term perspectives. What are the short- and long-term gains for solving the problem? Does a short-term solution take up resources that could be focused on producing a long-term solution?

Case study 3.5a   Eating and drinking in the library
The information service in a learned society had a problem with readers using the library to eat their sandwiches and read newspapers and journals. The effects of this behaviour were a noisy library, food and litter left on the table, and food marks on some publications. The issue was regularly brought up at library team meetings and also the information services user group meetings. Alison, the information services team leader for user services, decided to tackle this recurrent problem and used the different perspectives listed above to think through the issue with her team. Their key findings were:

1 The importance of the issue. Is the issue worthwhile resolving? There was a general consensus by the library staff and also the users' group that the problem was worth tackling. It was decided that Alison should attempt to solve the problem and that she should present her work to the ILS senior managers plus the user group.

2 Is it a recurrent or non-recurrent issue? It was a recurrent issue. Alison asked ILS help-desk staff to keep a record of the problem for a month. This would help her to assess the specific nature and extent of the problem.

3 Different stakeholder perspectives. Alison obtained feedback from all ILS staff; she asked the users' group for feedback too. In addition, she checked with the human resources department to see if there were any issues that she needed to consider from their perspective.

4 Identify ILS and organizational perspectives. Alison and the information services team considered the issue from both the ILS and organizational perspectives. One point that they were aware of was that the society was moving to larger premises in two years' time and this was likely to include a better restaurant and also social areas.

5 Identify long- and short-term perspectives. Alison and the information services team decided that they needed to identify a short-term solution and also to ensure that the issue was considered when they started planning to move into their new building.

As a result of this initial analysis from a number of different perspectives, Alison and the information services team went ahead with the following problem-solving process. This case study is followed up after the description of the problem-solving process.

Once you have considered the problem from a number of different perspectives and made a decision to go ahead and attempt to solve it then you may start the problem-solving process. This involves the stages outlined in Figure 3.6.

Initial analysis

The first stage in problem solving is to carry out an initial analysis. Asking a series of questions may facilitate this analysis:

- What is the problem?
- What are the key issues?
- Whose problem is it?
- Who needs to be involved in developing a solution?
- What resources are available?
- What constraints exist?
- Is the problem worth resolving?

At this stage, it is worthwhile asking these questions of different team members and also other colleagues, e.g. other team leaders or managers within the ILS. This

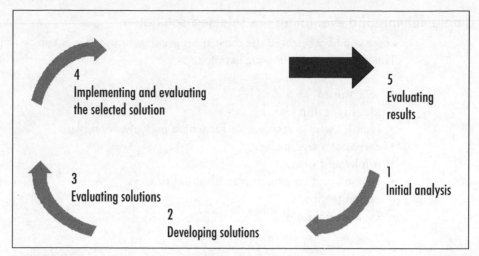

Figure 3.6 Problem-solving process

will help you to obtain a general overview of the problem.

Developing solutions

The second stage involves developing a range of potential solutions to the problem. This is likely to involve the team leader working with the team and other colleagues to gain a range of ideas. It may involve obtaining help from professional practice, e.g. literature, discussion lists, colleagues in other information and library services or in professional associations such as CILIP, ASLIB/IMI. It also involves using creativity techniques such as mind mapping, brainstorming, fishbone diagrams. For further information on these techniques, see Proctor (1999) or look at the website www.mindtools.com/.

Evaluating solutions

The next stage involves evaluating the potential solutions. There are many different ways of evaluating solutions and simple ones are to:

• identify the advantages and disadvantages of each solution
• use a group-decision process to evaluate each solution, e.g. each member of the team could be asked to champion a particular solution, and through the process of discussion and debate select the most appropriate solution
• identify a list of criteria for the perfect solution and weight each possible solution against the criteria, e.g. by scoring them out of 10
• select the most appropriate solution to the problem.

Implementing and evaluating the selected solution

Once you have selected the most appropriate solution then it can be implemented. This involves the following list of steps:

- select team
- identify action plan
- identify who is responsible for which part of action plan
- carry out a risk analysis
- implement plan
- monitor and control implementation process
- obtain feedback
- evaluate solution.

Case study 3.5b   Eating and drinking in the library (*continued*)

Initial analysis
This involved answering the following questions:

- What is the problem? Eating and drinking in the library, resulting in noise, litter and food marks on some publications.
- What are the key issues? Lack of space for staff to eat their lunches, noise and mess in library; it also looks unprofessional.
- Whose problem is it? Everyone who works or visits the society.
- Who needs to be involved in developing a solution? All ILS staff and also readers; also need to check with the human resources department.
- What resources are available? None.
- What constraints exist? We must come up with a solution that is acceptable to all parties. ILS senior managers and also the users' group must approve the solution before it can be implemented.
- Is the problem worth resolving? Yes. It is a constant point of tension between the users' group and ILS staff, and also between users.

Developing solutions
The team leader and team used brainstorming as a means of developing potential solutions. They came up with the following list of potential solutions:

1 Ban eating and drinking in the ILS.
2 Provide a special room for eating and drinking in the ILS and keep the newspapers and selected current periodicals in it.
3 Provide a special room for eating and drinking elsewhere in the building and keep the newspapers and selected current periodicals in it.

4 Provide a second set of newspapers and the most popular journals and allow these to be used by staff when they are eating their lunch. These could be made available either in the ILS or in a special room (see 2 and 3). Keep the first set of newspapers and journals as the archive set.
5 Ask for a cleaner to clean the ILS after the lunch break.

Evaluating solutions

Alison presented the range of options developed by her team to the ILS senior management team and the users' group. They discussed the advantages and disadvantages of each option. They decided that their preferred solution was to provide a special room for eating and drinking in the ILS and to provide newspapers but no journals in this room, and allow these to be used by readers when they are eating their lunch. They would also arrange for a cleaner to check and clean this room every afternoon at 2.30 p.m.

Implementing and evaluating the selected solution

Alison was given the task of implementing the decision. This involved the following steps:

1 Select team. The team with responsibility for implementing the solution was Alison and the information services team.
2 Identify action plan. They developed an action plan which included notifying readers of the change; producing new signs; liaising with the human resources department about the new working arrangements for the cleaner; and purchasing additional bins.
3 Identify who is responsible for which part of action plan. Each action was allocated to the most appropriate member of the team.
4 Carry out a risk analysis. Alison invited the health and safety officer to view the room and comment on their plans. He made a few suggestions about the wording of notices.
5 Implement plan. Alison and the information services team decided that they would introduce the change on the first day of the following month as this would be easy for everyone to remember.
6 Monitor and control implementation process. Alison and the information services team informally monitored the new arrangements. There were no problems and they found that all eating and drinking in the library was now restricted to this room.
7 Obtain feedback. This was achieved informally through a survey of users of the lunchtime reading room (as it became known in the society) and also via the users' group.
8 Evaluate solution. Alison and the information services team evaluated the solution and their findings were that it was a very successful innovation and had generated much goodwill within the society towards the library. Alison's manager commended her on the way in which she had tackled the problem and involved all parties in the solution.

Case study 3.5b demonstrates the value of using a problem-solving methodology. One of the strengths of this type of methodology is that it can sometimes help you to generate solutions that are not obvious. It also means that a large number of stakeholders are involved in the process.

Activity: Problem solving

Select a live problem from your workplace and use the problem-solving process to help you to identify and implement an appropriate solution to the problem. This process works best on a problem where there are a number of different solutions. Once you have carried out the problem-solving process then reflect on it. You could do this by asking yourself the following questions:

- What worked well?
- What could have been improved?
- What did I learn from the process?
- What will I do differently next time?

You could carry out this reflective process with your team or a mentor or trusted colleague.

Managing change

Nowadays all organizations face constant change. Change may be the result of a wide range of international, national, regional or local factors. Drivers for change are discussed in Chapter 1 and include globalization, changes in government policies, changes in communication and information technologies, the continuing information explosion and changes in the demands made on libraries and information services. The types of changes that face many organizations and that have a subsequent impact on their information and library services include:

- changes to organizational structures – downsizing, restructuring, mergers, fragmentation and franchising
- changes to markets – regionalization, globalization
- changes in law – international, European and national legislative frameworks
- changes in working practices, e.g. teleworking, computer conferencing, e-commerce
- changes in customers – increased expectations, more diverse customers, global customers, increased use of litigation
- changes in stakeholders – increased responsibility, increased outputs
- changes in expectations – demands for enhanced services and the provision of high-quality services.
- changes in the work of the ILS, e.g. increased involvement in training and development of end-users, increased emphasis on electronic resources

- increased competition for resources, e.g. within a local authority or company, or for research and development grants, e.g. European Social Fund monies
- increased emphasis on the need to demonstrate 'value for money' and the impact that the ILS makes within the organization
- new forms of working, e.g. working in multi-professional teams, working in virtual teams, working across traditional boundaries such as organizational boundaries
- the need to get to grips with new and developing forms of information and communications technologies
- the need to manage what is sometimes called the acceleration and compression of time.

Team leaders may find themselves on the receiving end of some of these changes and may need to support and steer their team through a series of changes. This can make for a turbulent environment as illustrated in Case study 3.6.

Case study 3.6   Working in a turbulent environment

Sumona has worked in an information department in the publishing industry in the UK for a number of years. She was recently made team leader. After only three months in this position she is seriously thinking about finding a less demanding job. She listed some of the changes that are currently facing her department:

- Takeover of company by an American publisher. This has led to uncertainty about the future of the department.
- Resignation of her manager who has moved to a competitor.
- Uncertainty about her own job. It will be evaluated and possibly regraded in the next two months.
- Introduction of flexible working is making it quite a challenge to staff the help desk from 9 a.m. to 5 p.m.
- A shift in the approach to publishing from a traditional print-base to multi-media. This has led to a shift in the work of the information department and a rise in the work that they now do on copyright issues.
- Long-term absence of a colleague due to stress.

This list indicates the extreme pressures that some information professionals work under. Sumona talked with her mentor (a senior manager from her 'old' company) about the pressures that she was experiencing. Her mentor, Jill, advised Sumona to carry on and to improve her position within the company by becoming more pro-active in the field of copyright and also by marketing her services to the technical authors with more aggression. Six months later Sumona's position was secure and she achieved a promotion. In addition, the new managers suggested that she considered taking a management qualification, an MBA, to help her to move to a more senior level within the company.

Two years later the company was taken over again and Sumona decided that she couldn't face another period of uncertainty. She retrained as a primary school teacher and is now teaching full time. She loves her new job and has become involved in developing the school's library resource centre.

Case study 3.6 indicates the levels of change and uncertainty that an individual team leader and team may be facing. There is no simple solution to this type of complex situation. It often requires a combination of stamina and political acumen. Understanding some of the psychological processes that individuals experience can be helpful as this provides some insights into what is happening when individuals experience change at work.

Many people feel apprehensive about going through a change process and they may go through a psychological process that is similar to that experienced in bereavement. Individual responses to change typically involve a number of distinct phases as shown in Figure 3.7.

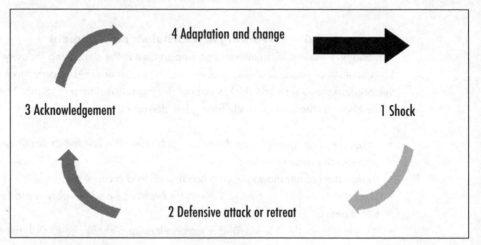

Figure 3.7 Individual responses to change

The first phase is one of shock and this is likely to be signalled by individuals feeling overwhelmed by the news and responding with panic, feelings of helplessness, numbness and shock. This phase may last minutes, hours, days or weeks. This is then often followed by what is called a defensive attack or retreat where people may attempt to maintain old structures and avoid their new reality. This stage is sometimes accompanied by feelings of indifference, euphoria or anger. Again, this stage may last from minutes to weeks. The next stage is the one where individuals begin to acknowledge the situation and face reality. This stage may be accompanied by feelings of indifference or bitterness. At this stage, some people may decide that it is better for them to leave their employer and find a new job. The final stage is one of adaptation and change, and here individuals begin to rebuild their lives and gradually gain their confidence and self esteem in the new situation.

It is worthwhile remembering that individuals are likely to move through these phases in their own time and this means that within a team there may be individuals at each of the different phases. In addition, some staff may still be engaged or 'stuck' in this cycle as a result of previous changes within the ILS. In this situation, as team leader, you will be managing the current responses to change as well as responses to previous changes.

The different strategies required for managing and supporting people through change are summarized in Figure 3.8. As a team leader an awareness of these responses to change is important because at different stages you will need to focus on different aspects of the change process. For example when staff are experiencing shock it is important to focus on the communication processes and to provide lots of opportunity to explain the current situation. You will need to remember that they may not

Be adaptable Delegate Monitor Support Mentor Encourage flexibility of approach Value considered risk taking	Provide a vision for the future Explain and keep on explaining Talk to individuals Communicate, communicate, communicate Listen, listen, listen Give reassurance Put the change into perspective Do not give out too much information – keep it simple Handle people with great sensitivity Keep your feet on the ground Be available
Phase 4 **Adjustment**	**Phase 1** **Shock**
Phase 3 **Acknowledgement**	**Phase 2** **Defensive attack or retreat**
Provide more detailed information Keep listening Evaluate options Support realistic ideas and strategies You don't have to provide ALL the answers Provide direction not control Involve as many people as possible in the planning process Acknowledge positively people's efforts	Don't panic! Don't take staff reactions personally Keep listening Allow people to let off steam Highlight the positives Keep meetings to the point Don't get hooked into win/lose situation Don't get hooked into critical parent Use a wide range of strategies Include people who appear to have 'switched off' from the situation

Figure 3.8 Managing and supporting people through change
Note: Original source of this diagram is unknown.

remember everything that has been communicated to them and so you are likely to need to repeat the message, perhaps many times, and give lots of reassurance.

In some situations the team leader may be working through this psychological process themselves. For example you may be asked to manage the closure of a library with very little notice. This may mean that you are experiencing shock at the same time as your colleagues. This is an extremely challenging situation because you must provide leadership and guidance at a time when you are experiencing a variety of emotions. This type of situation requires emotional intelligence and it is vital that you obtain support and guidance, e.g. from a mentor, and this is explored in Chapter 10.

Summary

The chapter considers some of the characteristics of confident team leaders. The assertiveness model offers a useful framework for exploring, understanding and managing situations in the workplace. In contrast, the concept of emotional intelligence offers a framework for exploring the emotional side of leading and working in teams. Team leaders are regularly asked to solve problems: using a problem-solving framework helps to ensure that the problem is tackled in a logical manner and that all the appropriate stakeholders are involved in developing and implementing the most appropriate solution. Nowadays team leaders frequently work in a turbulent environment and may be involved in managing change. This often involves managing our own responses to change as well as supporting and leading team members. Again a model and a framework can help team leaders understand and respond to individual reactions to change.

References

Back, K. and Back, K. (1999) *Assertiveness at Work*, 3rd edn, London, McGraw-Hill.

Dickson, A. (2002) *A Woman in Your Own Right*, London, Quartet Books.

Goleman, D. (1995) *Emotional Intelligence*, New York, Bantam.

O'Connor, J. and Seymour, J. (1993) *Introducing Neuro-linguistic Programming*, Dartford, Aquarian Press.

Proctor, T. (1999) *Creative Problem Solving for Managers*, London, Routledge.

4   Motivation

Introduction

This chapter presents some common motivation theories that help to explain some of the ways in which team leaders can motivate their team. The final section of the chapter covers motivational drivers that may be used to help motivate individuals or a whole team. These motivational drivers are particularly useful because they provide insights into the ways in which we can influence individuals or the whole team through our use of language. This chapter includes a range of case studies and examples. Case study 4.1 is a long one and this is referred to in the subsequent sections on motivation theory.

Introduction to motivation

A motivated team is essential if you want to provide a high-quality information and library service. Motivated teams are a pleasure to work with and mean that, as team leader, you look forward to going to work in the morning. In contrast, demotivated teams are challenging and require a careful development process if they are to change. If you ask individuals about what motivates them at work then you are likely to obtain a range of responses including:

- being able to pay the mortgage and other bills
- doing a good job
- helping people
- learning new things
- doing an interesting job
- developing my career
- working with friendly people
- not doing the same thing every day
- being able to make my own decisions.

Understanding what motivates individuals and how to improve their motivation is vital to being an effective team leader.

Case study 4.1 The new team leader

The accessions team in a public library was made up of five team members: two part-time clerical assistants (Joan and Jane); two administrative officers (Clare and Tom); and a qualified librarian (Andrea). The team had experienced a number of difficulties in the past three years including loss of a treasured team leader due to cancer; two new team leaders who only stayed for nine months each; change in their work, i.e. rise in purchase of DVDs and CDs and fall in the number of books purchased; threat of closure of department with the idea that acquisitions would be outsourced. Morale in the department was very low and this was illustrated by high rates of absence due to sickness, errors in their work and slow processing of new stock. In addition, the department had developed the reputation for being rude and unfriendly over the phone.

Valerie was appointed as the new team leader and was new to the library service though she had extensive experience of working in public libraries. Valerie tackled the problem in a number of different ways.

In her first week

- Valerie had an informal meeting with each member of the team and asked them what they liked about their job and what they didn't like. In this way she began to get to know each member of the team and the main issues.
- Valerie met with the whole team. She asked them to carry out a SWOT analysis (see Chapter 1) on the department. She also asked the team for their ideas of ways of improving their working lives.
- She talked with other managers about the accessions team and their work within the public library system.
- Valerie spent much of her time in the department working with the team as a way of getting to know them and their work. She presented a positive role model giving positive feedback to staff. She talked about herself and her intention to stay long term in the department.

In her first month

- Valerie met with the director of the service and talked about staff fears for the future of the department. They explored the idea of expanding the work of the department to take on board additional duties, i.e. booking of meeting rooms and computers, dealing with e-mail queries. This would enrich their jobs and also mean that if the department did close then staff would be better placed to move into other parts of the service. Valerie took this idea back to the team and individuals were interested in developing their roles. They were pleased that Valerie had talked directly with the director and felt that 'she was on their side'. Valerie emphasized the value of developing their roles as a means of ensuring their employability and agreed that additional training would be required.
- Valerie continued with her 'hands-on' approach to working with her team. She identified a number of ways of improving the flow of work within the department and

these were implemented by staff. Andrea said 'I've been suggesting this for years' and overall staff were pleased with the changes.

- One concern expressed by staff in their first team meeting was the state of their toilet. It hadn't been decorated for years and was a miserable and shabby room. Valerie put pressure onto the estates department and they agreed to refurbish the toilet within six weeks. Staff were delighted with this news though one person, Joan, didn't believe that it would happen.
- Another grumble in the department was that they did not have easy access to drinking water and they had to walk to another department if they wanted to use a bottled water dispenser. Staff interpreted this as the managers in the library service seeing them as second class citizens. Valerie investigated this situation and discovered that no one had requested bottled water in the accessions department, so she put in a request. Three weeks later a water dispenser was placed in the department.
- An external trainer led a session on 'putting customers first'. Although staff had been very negative about the idea of this event they actually enjoyed it and said that 'it was very practical and useful'.
- Sometimes when Valerie returned to the team's work room after a meeting there was an immediate silence as if the staff had been discussing her and the changes. Valerie ignored these silences.
- Valerie introduced a 'cake and tea' ritual for team members' birthdays and other special days.
- Valerie drafted an action plan that included introducing a weekly team meeting; agreeing individual objectives with each member of staff; introducing some training sessions within the department; and talking with the human resources department regarding absences.

In her third month
- Morale in the team had improved and absence due to sickness had dropped significantly.
- A number of training sessions had taken place and these were well received.
- The toilet had been redecorated.
- A project had been set up with the reference department to manage a pilot in which some members of the acquisitions team answered the e-mail queries.
- Room and IT bookings were now being handled by the acquisitions department and two clerical staff who dealt with these queries were very positive about this new aspect of their work.
- One of the clerical assistants, Joan, resigned as she felt the work was becoming too pressurized and involved too much training. She said that 'she had had too much change at work and wanted things to stay the same'.
- Staff were beginning to talk about changing the name of their department and wanted this to be discussed at the next team meeting.

This example, based on a real-life situation, illustrates that it takes months to begin to change morale. What appeared to work in this case was the professionalism of the new team leader who listened to staff members and took on board and sorted out some of their issues, e.g. the dingy toilet. She demonstrated her competence by her hands-on approach to her work and her understanding of the issues involved in the work of the department. In addition, she saw the department within the wider context of the service and involved other teams in the solutions. Valerie accepted the loss of Joan from the department and felt that the possibility of obtaining a new recruit would help move the team forward.

Eighteen months after taking on this role Valerie said:

> It took me three months to get the ball rolling and to begin to improve morale. The first three months were hard work and I often felt as if I was treading on egg shells. I sometimes dreaded coming to work. It suddenly began to get easier. In part this was due to Joan leaving the team as I realized, in hindsight, that she had been very negative about work and me. However, all the small changes and larger changes did have a positive impact and after six months I felt as if we'd turned a corner. The last year has been much more positive. We have changed our name to the resources department as this takes into account our new roles with respect to room and computer bookings, and also answering many e-mail queries. Room bookings and computer bookings are constantly rising and Clare and Tom are proud of the statistics of this service and keep showing me charts to show how much work they do. The project with the reference department has worked well and we now, as a matter of routine, respond to basic e-mail queries. This has helped remotivate the team and integrate them into the whole service. Fear of outsourcing has gone away as staff feel that if that was to happen then they could easily be transferred into another part of the library service.

Psychology of motivation

The management literature provides an extensive set of theories and models of motivation. These are useful in providing some general guidelines and pointers for motivating your team. However, it is really important to remember that individuals are motivated on an individual basis; people are complex, and we don't always know what is happening in someone's private life and this may have a big impact on their behaviour at work.

Motivation theories and individual needs

One set of motivational theories is called 'content' approaches and these are based on the idea that individuals have clearly defined needs and that team leaders can motivate their team by addressing these needs. The most famous of the content approaches is the motivation theory developed by Maslow in 1954 (see Mullins,

2006). Maslow developed the idea of a pyramid or hierarchy of needs and suggested that people are motivated to move up the hierarchy but will only do so as each level of needs is met. He suggested that ultimately people are motivated to achieve self-actualization. The different levels of his hierarchy are shown in Figure 4.1 and these are linked with the activities introduced by the team leader, Valerie, in Case study 4.1.

Maslow's hierarchy of needs	Ways in which the need is satisfied	Examples from case study
Self-actualization	Autonomous working; working on interesting and challenging projects; opportunities to progress; opportunities to innovate and be creative	Introduction of new projects; new training opportunities
Self-esteem	Recognition for completing good-quality work	Regular praise; involvement in consultations and discussions about possible changes
Social needs	Acceptance as part of a team; working relationships; friendships	Regular team meetings; celebrations of birthdays and other special days; development of working with other teams, e.g. reference team
Safety and security needs	Economic security; physical safety; emotional safety; absence of threatening or bullying individuals or environment	Expansion of work roles to mitigate against fear of outsourcing
Physiological needs	Water, food, fresh air, warmth	Provision of bottled water; redecoration of toilet

Figure 4.1 Maslow's hierarchy of needs

This motivational theory has been criticized. For example it is based on western ideas about individuals and motivation, and does not take into account motivating factors in other cultures: it assumes individual self-fulfilment whereas in some cultures people are motivated by collective rather than individual goals. The model presents a heierarchy of needs but this is probably an oversimplification and individuals may be operating at a number of levels at once, e.g. someone may ignore a physiological need such as hunger in order to complete a piece of work as a means of enhancing their self-esteem. Despite these criticisms, Maslow's theory does offer some insights into motivation in the workplace. Some writers, e.g. Norwood

(1999), have used the theory to describe the different kinds of information that individuals require at each level. This is illustrated in Table 4.1.

Table 4.1 Motivation and information requirements

Maslow's hierarchy of needs	Information requirements
Self-actualization	Information about career development possibilities; information about opportunities to take part in challenging projects and/or new job opportunities
Self-esteem needs	Feedback about quality of work; information about training and development, and quality standards at work
Social needs	Information about colleagues and working arrangements that enable people to work together
Safety and security needs	Helping information, e.g. information relating to job security, health and safety information
Physiological needs	Coping information, e.g. location of toilets, access to water machine, breaks.

Another model of motivation was developed by Herzberg (described in Mullins, 2006) who identified the 'satisfiers' and 'dissatisfiers', or hygiene factors, that affect our motivation at work. If our hygiene factors are not met then we will be dissatisfied at work. However, these hygiene factors don't motivate us and it is the satisfiers that will ultimately help to motivate individuals at work. These factors are summarized in Table 4.2. The items marked with an asterisk are those addressed by the team leader, Valerie, in the case study presented at the start of this chapter. The distribution of the asterisks indicates that she addressed both dissatisfiers and satisfiers at the same time. There were some dissatisfiers, i.e. basic salary, that were not within her remit. The case study illustrates that addressing a range of dissatisfiers and satisfiers can have a significant impact on motivation.

Table 4.2 Herzberg's model of motivation

Dissatisfiers (hygiene factors)	Satisfiers (motivators)
Working conditions	The work itself *
Physical environment *	Responsibility
Basic salary and bonuses	Recognition *
Working practices *	Working relationships *
Job security *	Possibilities for promotion

Managing the people processes at work

Another set of motivational factors comprises 'process' approaches. They are described in Mullins (2006) and include:

- Expectancy theory. Concerned with the amount of effort someone puts into their work and their expected reward, e.g. in terms of pay or promotion.
- Equity theory. Concerned with the way in which individuals compare themselves with others in terms of the amount of effort they put into their work and the rewards they receive for this work.
- Goal-setting theory. Concerned with the goals that individuals set for themselves and the suggestion that the more challenging the goal then the better their performance at work.

These process approaches to motivation are important for team leaders because they serve as a reminder that individuals expect their rewards at work to be in line with the amount of effort they put into the work; that they need to be treated fairly; and that goal setting can be an important way of motivating staff as illustrated in Case studies 4.2, 4.3 and 4.4.

Case study 4.2   Expectancy theory

Peter worked in a special library in the publishing industry and his team leader, Jane, suggested that he took on additional responsibilities. He agreed to this and it meant that he worked for longer hours, frequently had to travel to the company's head office (meaning a 14-hour day) and was under much more pressure. Jane said that if he carried out this extra responsbility for 12 months then he would be promoted to a higher grade. There was no formal documentation of this arrangement. Eleven months later Jane left the company and the new team leader, John, was unable to fulfil Jane's promise to Peter. The end result was that Peter felt that his additional efforts had not reaped the expected reward leaving him disenchanted with the company and demotivated in his work.

Case study 4.3   Equity theory

Barbara worked in the library of the education division of an international computing company. Her qualifications included a master's degree in information science plus five years' experience in special library work. She set up the library from scratch and after six months it was firmly established within the division and well used by a wide range of staff. In casual conversations with colleagues Barbara discovered that the clerical officer, Denise, whose role was to book customers onto company training courses and whose qualifications were minimal, was earning an extra £3000 per year. She felt that this was unfair and that her qualifications and ability to deal with high-level work and complex queries were not being recognized within the company. She contacted the human resources department and asked for a pay review on the grounds that she was being unfairly treated in comparison with other staff whose work was at a lower level than hers. The human resources department said that individual salaries were confidential and that they wouldn't review Barbara's salary. Three months later she left the company.

Case study 4.4   Goal setting theory

Dilys was team leader in an academic library which was moving to a new building over the summer vacation. Dilys and her team worked out how long it would take to process and move 100,000 books and set weekly targets for the movement of books. The team were proud of the targets and managed to achieve them throughout the summer period. In the last week of the move, all team members doubled their targets as they were so keen to complete the job a few days early 'to prove that it could be done'. When talking about this achievement it was clear that all team members felt proud that they had achieved *their* targets. The significant factor appears to be that they had set and agreed their own targets rather than accepting a target handed down to them by senior managers.

Motivating individuals and the whole team

The purpose of this section is to consider practical approaches to motivating others. An important development in motivational theory is motivational traits (or meta programmes). This development took place in the 1980s as part of the field of knowledge called neuro-linguistic programming (NLP). These motivational traits have been written about by a number of authors including Charvet (1997) and Knight (2002). They are underlying patterns or ways of systematically dealing with the outside world. The concept of underlying motivational patterns is based on the idea that individuals have their own preferences in the ways that they look at and filter what happens in the outside world.

The motivational traits are systematic and habitual within a particular context. For example, what holds our attention in an ILS environment may be different from what we pay attention to while we are on holiday or socializing with friends. No value judgements are implied by these motivational traits, none is 'right' or 'better' in itself. However, in a specific context and with a particular outcome in mind, some motivational traits are more useful than others. As a team leader or manager you can identify a person's motivational traits through their language and behaviour. The key to uncovering someone's motivational traits is to:

- observe how they behave and what is important to them
- listen to *how* they answer the question rather than *what* they say
- observe how they structure and write e-mails or reports.

The motivational traits provide a framework and explanation about what people say and do in a work environment. They provide team leaders and supervisors with a series of strategies for working with people. They can be used to:

- recognize why some things work for some people and not for others
- alter an approach that isn't working
- use appropriate language when talking to individuals or the whole team
- develop greater personal flexibility
- build on the motivation of groups/individuals
- understand why someone is finding something particularly difficult
- learn about your own style and its effectiveness.

The following motivational traits are particularly relevant in a work context:

- moving towards/away
- possibility/necessity
- self/other
- options/procedures
- same/difference.

Each of these categories of motivational traits describes behaviour on a continuum with one trait at one end and another trait at the other end. This is illustrated in Figure 4.2.

Figure 4.2 Motivational trails

These common motivational traits are outlined below and each paragraph describes a particular motivational trait and then gives detailed information about how to recognize the pattern and how to use it in the workplace (adapted from Garrett, 1997). If this is the first time you have come across these ideas then you may find the amount of detail presented overwhelming. My suggestion is that you skim through the explanations now and then choose one pattern a week and explore it.

Moving towards or away from

This motivational trait is important as it suggests a basic orientation in how individuals are motivated. Some people will be motivated towards a goal, e.g.

completing a piece of work, promotion or gaining the respect of colleagues. Others are motivated away from problems, e.g. they don't want mistakes in their work, they will work hard at preventing failure, they will think about what may go wrong in a problem and work to prevent problems or failure. Some people are a mixture of moving towards/moving away from or moving away from/moving towards motivational patterns. Another way of describing this motivational trait is in terms of a carrot (moving towards) or stick (moving away from). This pattern is summarized in Table 4.3.

Table 4.3   Moving towards and moving away from motivational traits

	Moving towards	**Moving away from**
Overview	People who demonstrate this motivational trait are likely to have clear goals in mind and they want to work towards their goals. They may be over-optimistic and have trouble identifying problems.	People who demonstrate this motivational trait are likely to focus on problems. They are motivated to solve problems and they may have trouble keeping focused on goals.
How to recognize this pattern	These people tend to use positive language and speak from an 'I' position. They will talk about benefits, achievements, goals, etc.	These people will not have a clear goal in mind. They will talk about things they want to avoid, use passive language, and talk about problems.
How to work with them	Work together to create goals and objectives. Talk about the goals that the team is working towards. Use incentives rather than threats.	Get them to identify problems and ways of solving them. Encourage them to look ahead for any potential problem areas. Identify the problems that may arise if work isn't completed to the required standard.

As a team leader it is worthwhile thinking about setting goals to help motivate individuals who present a moving towards trait and also identifying problems or consequences that will help individuals who are motivated away from problems. Table 4.3 provides some guidance on working with this particular motivational trait.

Possibility/necessity

This motivational trait helps to give some useful insights into an individual's general outlook at work. People who have a strong possibility driver will be interested in seeing possibilities and new ways of improving services and establishing new ways of working. For example, in Case study 4.1 Valerie saw new possibilities for the team, such as carrying out room and computer bookings and also responding to e-mail queries. In contrast, people with a necessity driver will often feel that they have no choice, e.g. they must do the work that they have always done and that there are no possibilities for change. Table 4.4 provides some guidance on working with this particular motivational trait.

Table 4.4   Possibility and necessity motivational traits

	Possibility	Necessity
Overview	People who are focused on possibilities tend to be positive, enthusiastic and keen to try new things.	These people often feel that they have no choice. They are not looking to get anything out of the work or life. They want to survive it.
How to recognize this pattern	They will tell their team leader what they want to do and are interested in new possibilities, choices and options. They will talk about doing things and use words like 'wish', 'want', 'possibility', 'can do'.	They will often give evidence of not being in control of their work. They will not see options that exist within an organization. They will use words like 'must', 'have to', 'need', 'should'.
How to work with them	Help them to see new opportunities for improving practice in the workplace, learning or change. Help them to see how they can apply their new ideas or what they have learnt. Don't tie them down to a rigid set of instructions. Use words like 'choice', 'possible', 'different', 'alternatives'.	Fully explain anything new. Be highly structured and systematic in explaining what is required at work. Provide options in a very structured manner. Use words like 'evidence', 'known', 'correct', 'right way'.

Self/other

This motivational trait helps to give some useful insights into people's ways of relating to themselves and others. People who have a strong self-driver are often viewed as 'selfish' and will tend to see the world from their own perspective and not think about the needs of others. In contrast, someone with a very strong 'other' driver will tend to focus on the needs of others and this is likely to be at the expense of themselves. People with a strong 'other' driver will often prioritize relationships and may find it hard to work with someone if there is not an exchange of information about themselves and their feelings. Team leaders who have a strong 'self' driver may find it hard to motivate team members with a strong 'other' driver unless they make efforts to get to know their team members and spend some time on day-to-day exchanges. Table 4.5 provides some guidance on working with this particular motivational trait.

Table 4.5 Self and other motivational traits

	Self	Other
Overview	People who are very self-oriented. They pay a lot of attention to their own thoughts and feelings.	These people are very sensitive to others and quickly establish relationships with new team members. They will quickly pick up on the feelings, needs and wants of others.
How to recognize this pattern	They tend not to show emotions. They tend to pick up on what is said rather than how it is said. They often do not have highly developed people skills. They don't reveal much emotion on their faces.	They tend to show emotions. They will respond to what is said and also how it is said. They will be aware of how others are responding and feeling. During meetings, they will look around the room to check others out.
How to work with them	Keep the input focused on specifics. Show them you understand them. Give them space. Don't try too hard to build a relationship with them. Do be very clear about what is being said.	Build a relationship that includes an explicit emotional or personal element. Be expressive in communicating with them. Emphasize the people side of the work. Talk about how others are involved in the work.

Options/procedures

This motivational trait helps to give an insight into someone's approaches to work. People who have a strong 'option' driver will like to make choices about what they do each day and how they carry out their work. These are the people who travel to work by lots of different routes. People with a strong 'procedures' driver are extremely comfortable following set procedures and may get annoyed if the procedure doesn't deal with exceptions. When giving instructions people with an 'options' driver are likely to treat the instruction as an option and may well ignore it and produce their own way of working. In contrast, someone who has a strong 'procedures' driver will happily follow the procedure and ask for help if they come up with an unusual situation. Table 4.6 provides some guidance on working with this particular motivational trait.

Table 4.6 Options and procedures motivational traits

	Options	Procedures
Overview	These people love choice and will like to have a range of possible options available to them.	These people prefer to follow a set procedure and if a procedure is not available they will design one or (preferably) ask their team leader to design a procedure.
How to recognize this pattern	These people will look for options and choices in their work. They will search out new ways of carrying out their work. If they are given a procedure to follow then they are likely to change it, i.e. develop their own option. They will use words like 'option' and 'choice'.	These people will follow established procedure and they will ask for a procedure if one isn't offered. They answer the question 'why?' by telling 'how' it happened. They will tell a story by telling the order in which something happened.
How to work with them	Offer choices and options. Ask them to come up with alternatives. Use phrases such as 'the options are . . .' or 'you can choose . . .'. Treat their variation on your instructions with respect.	Offer them clear procedures and guidelines. Don't offer them too many choices (it causes overload). Use phrases such as 'the rule is . . .' 'the right way . . .' and 'first . . . then . . . finally . . .'. Give them time to tell their 'procedural' stories.

Same/difference

This motivational trait helps to give an insight into the amount of change people are comfortable with. People who have a strong 'sameness' driver like work to remain the same. These are the people who don't like change and often like to remain in the same job and working with the same people for a number of years. In contrast, people with a strong 'difference' driver love change and may change their jobs and type of work at regular intervals. These are the people who often get involved in project work that by definition involves change and innovation. When introducing change to people with a 'sameness' driver it is important to emphasize what is going to stay the same, e.g. working in the same building with the same team and the same customers, and to minimize the parts that are going to change. Table 4.7 provides some guidance on working with this particular motivational trait.

Table 4.7   Same and difference motivational traits

	Same	Difference
Overview	These people tend not to like change and find it hard to adapt to new skills, techniques and ideas. They are unlikely to initiate change. They often stay in the same job or ILS for a long time.	These people love change, new ideas and innovation. They change jobs or organizations frequently and need a constant spur and stimulus.
How to recognize this pattern	They will use words like 'same', 'similar', 'common'. They will be conservative with new ideas. They will have been in the same job doing the same activities for a long time.	They will look towards the next steps and the future, and they will not want to dwell on the past. They will quickly accept new ideas and want to make changes at work. They may regularly be looking for a new job.
How to work with them	Emphasize similarities in the new ideas or working practices and the old ones. Show areas of commonality. Show that you are both working to the same goals. Build upon what they already know.	Show them how new skills and ideas will change things. Emphasize change and difference. Use words like 'new', 'innovative', 'unique', 'never been done before'.

Case study 4.5 illustrates how the idea of motivational traits can be used in practice. Each specific phrase that relates to a specific motivational trait is provided with a number and at the end of the case study a key is provided to link the numbers with a specific motivational trait.

Case study 4.5   Using motivational traits in practice

Donna is the team leader of an information skills team in a large academic library and she has the task of explaining to her team that they will be merging with the IT trainers' team to form a new student support staff. This is how Donna presents the idea to take into account the dominant motivational traits of her team.

Thanks for coming to this meeting. I know that lots of rumours have been spreading about the restructuring. I'm now able to let you know what had been decided for our team. We will all remain working together and in the same area of information skills work (1) and we will also be working with the IT trainers. We all know the IT trainers very well and have worked with them over the years on various projects. Merging the two teams makes sense as it means that we can keep on working in the same way (2) and also possibly find new ways of working and improving our services to students (3). Our priorities are going to stay the same, i.e. enhancing students' information skills (4), and one opportunity this gives us is that by working in a team with the IT trainers we will be able to offer integrated programmes and get away from some of the problems caused last year (5). Overall, I'm pleased with the decision. It means that we can all remain working together (6) and I'm sure that we can keep on providing super support to students (7).

1 – sameness, 2 – sameness, 3 – difference, 4 – sameness, 5 – away from,
6 – sameness, 7 – sameness and also towards.

The team leader of the IT trainers, Lynn, held a meeting with her team and she presented the same scenario in a slightly different way and one that took into account the dominant meta programmes in her team.

Thanks for coming to this meeting. I know that lots of rumours have been spreading about the restructuring. I'm now able to let you know what has been decided for our team. You've all been hoping for change (8) and I'm pleased to say that there are some significant changes following the review (9). The main change (10) is that we are going to be merging with the information skills team and we'll form a new team. Although our main responsibilities remain the same (11) we will have additional work and the chance to develop a more integrated way of working (12). We'll have new goals and I hope that we'll get the chance to work with every student on the campus (13). My role is going to change too. I'll no longer be your team leader but I'll still be working in the team as my new role is that of project manager for the new IRIS project (14). Overall, I'm very positive about the merger. It will bring us lots of new opportunities for working with the information skills team and I think it will help us to make a real impact on students' skills (15).

8 – difference, 9 – difference, 10 – difference, 11 – sameness,
12 – sameness/difference, 13 – towards, 14 – difference, 15 – towards.

Case study 4.5 illustrates that motivational traits can be used to help us to organize and structure communications as a means of motivating others. If you do not know the people to whom you are speaking or if you are speaking to a large group then it is a good idea to cover as many motivational traits as possible in your presentation.

Activity: Practise using motivational traits

Select one of the motivational traits and the next time you introduce a new idea to your team, e.g. at a meeting, present the idea using both ends of the continuum for the trait. Notice the impact this has on your team.

Common questions about motivational traits

The following are some common questions and answers about motivational traits:

1   **How many motivational traits are there?**

There are a large number of motivational traits. Some people say that there are more than 72 of them. However, the ones presented here have been found by the author to be particularly useful when working with others in a team.

2   **This is all very complicated. How can I recognize the motivational traits in my team?**

Select one of the traits and think about it in relation to individuals. However, remember that people are very sophisticated and that this is a rough guide.

When dealing with a group of people remember that different people will display different motivational traits. If you think about the motivational traits before going into a meeting and introducing a new idea then it is possible to take into account a wide range of motivational traits in the way in which you talk. The more motivational traits you cover in the ways in which you talk or write to a group of people the more likely you are to influence them.

3   **You have presented the motivational traits as a dichotomy. Isn't this an oversimplification?**

Yes it is. Each pair of motivational traits is actually a continuum and individuals may be motivated at different positions on the continuum depending on the trait and the specific context.

The actual distribution of these motivational traits was researched and identified by Shellet Rose Charvet (1999) and a summary is presented in Figure 4.3. Note that the motivational traits are not grouped together in the way they are presented in the figure and different people will have different combinations of motivational traits. For example, one person may have the following combination of motivational traits: moving towards, self, procedure, same/difference. Another person may have the combination: away, necessity, other/self, procedure, same. The arrow suggests that there is to be a continuum across specific motivational traits.

4   **How do motivational traits influence the ways in which we communicate with others?**

Individuals will tend to communicate with others by emphasizing their own traits. For example, I have a natural tendency to emphasize moving towards goals, the different possibilities that arise in a situation, a mixture of self and others, options, and I love difference. These are my own preferred motivational traits in a work

←	→	
moving towards (40%)	moving towards/away away/moving towards (20%)	away (40%)
possibility (40%)	possibility/necessity necessity/possibility (20%)	necessity (40%)
self (40%)	self/other other/self (20%)	other (40%)
option (40%)	option/procedure procedure/option (20%)	procedure (40%)
same (60%)	same/difference difference/same (30%)	difference (10%)

Figure 4.3 Distribution of motivational traits

context. However, if I am presenting information and ideas to others then I work hard at covering the perspectives of people with different motivational trait preferences to myself. This helps to build rapport and also motivate and influence others.

5 Isn't there a danger of labelling and stereotyping people?

Yes, there is. It is important to remember that people are sophisticated and that our motivational traits change according to our context and also over time. For example, my drivers or motivational traits when I am a team member are different to those when I am dealing with a customer at a help desk. In addition, my motivational traits change over time, e.g. as a result of different work and other life experiences.

6 What is the research evidence for motivational traits?

The main research that this section is based on was carried out by Shellet Rose Charvet (1997) and this model is widely used in management training and other communication skills programmes.

Activity: Team development process using motivational traits

As part of a team building activity you could introduce the idea of motivational traits to your team. Present the five common motivational traits outlined above to your team. It is helpful to do this using PowerPoint slides and to emphasize that the traits represent a continuum. For each trait, ask individual members to stand up and move around so that they position themselves along a continuum that represents that trait. You may find it helpful to ask them to comment on what they like about their position. Remember there are no good or bad motivational traits and that each one has its own strengths. You will find that different people stand in different positions for each motivational trait. This helps to indicate how your team is made up of diverse people each bringing their strengths to the team. I have used this activity in practice in team-building events and people tend to enjoy it. They like moving about and discussing their positions and what motivates them.

Summary

This chapter provides general guidelines on motivating team members. Theoretical models of motivation are helpful because they indicate some of the ways in which individuals are motivated at work. The concept of motivational traits is helpful as it provides a means of helping to motivate and influence others at work. Effective team leaders are people who get to know their staff and what 'makes them tick'. They get to know and respect team members taking into account their diverse needs.

References

Charvet, S. R. (1997) *Words That Change Minds: mastering the language of influence*, Dubugue IO, Kendall/Hunt Publishing Company.

Garrett, T. (1997) *The Effective Delivery of Training Using NLP*, London, Kogan Page.

Knight, S. (2002) *NLP at Work*, rev. edn, London, Nicholas Brealey.

Maslow, A. (1954) *Motivation and Personality*, New York NY, Harper.

Mullins, L. (2006) *Management and Organisational Behaviour*, 7th edn, London, FT/Prentice Hall.

Norwood, G. (1999) Maslow's Hierarchy of Needs, *The Truth Vectors* (Part I), www.deepermind.com/20maslow.htm (accessed 12 May 2006).

5   Managing the work

Introduction

This chapter is concerned with managing the work in your team. This includes creating an appropriate working environment so that the information and library service both looks professional and is also a pleasant working environment. This chapter considers ways of managing both types of work experienced in an ILS: routine work and project work. It also considers issues relevant to both routine and project work, i.e. delegating tasks, giving instructions, giving feedback, setting goals and monitoring and reviewing performance.

Managing the work environment

The physical work environment, i.e. the organization and layout of the public and staff areas in the ILS, will have an impact on everyone coming into the service. Individuals will judge your ILS on the basis of what they see. If they come into an environment where everything looks tidy, notices are up-to-date and welcoming, and there is the sense of stepping into a professional workspace then they are likely to feel positive about the ILS. Conversely, if the ILS looks disorganized with out-of-date notices, old computers cluttering up corners, dying plants in dark corners, staff desks heaped with piles of paper and used coffee cups, then potential readers are unlikely to feel confident about the quality of service. In addition, there are health and safety factors to be taken into account in organizing the work environment: a well organized and tidy environment is likely to be a safe environment.

Managing the work environment involves everyone taking responsibility for their own working space and the public areas of the ILS. Many team leaders ensure that individual members of staff have responsibility for specific aspects of maintaining the physical environment and tasks such as tidying book shelves, notice boards, organizing and maintaining the stationery store, and checking that computers are working.

Ways of providing a professional-looking ILS involve ensuring:

- tidy and up-to-date notice boards
- effective and up-to-date guiding
- temporary guiding produced to a good standard
- tidy shelves

- reader areas checked and tidied at regular intervals
- public computers and printers checked regularly
- tidy and uncluttered help desks
- everything labelled and in the most appropriate place
- absence of food and drink in all public areas
- providing a 'trophy' wall where photographs, e.g. of visitors to the service, awards and other accolades are displayed to anyone coming to the service.

In addition, it is important to ensure that staff offices or workspaces are well organized and this involves:

- agreeing ground rules with the team regarding ways of maintaining a pleasant working environment
- providing sufficient filing cabinets and other storage spaces
- ensuring that all desk surfaces are kept tidy with clutter reduced to a minimum
- thinking about the layout so that there are spaces where staff can work on 'quiet' tasks away from phone calls, photocopiers and other interruptions
- a staff notice board where rotas and other important information are displayed
- providing a 'trophy' wall where feedback and praise is highlighted. For example, one special library known to the author uses photo frames to display feedback from customers. The team leader says that it helps to promote positive morale.
- setting aside time to tidy up the staff environment and get rid of clutter, e.g. on a monthly and annual basis.

Analysing the work

The next aspect of thinking about the working environment is to consider the type of work that the team is involved in. Traditional ILS work involves working in 'process' teams where staff undertake routine and standardized activities or tasks such as issuing books, carrying out a database search or producing current-awareness bulletins. In contrast, project work involves taking on tasks that are new to the team, involve innovation and changes to the status quo. The features of these two types of working are summarized in Table 5.1.

Some team leaders organize their department so that process work, e.g. specific tasks, is carried out at specific desks and when someone is working on that task then they will work in the location assigned for the task. In contrast, project work may involve people coming together regularly for meetings and this means that they need access to a meeting room or a workspace where they won't disrupt people working on routine operations. It is worthwhile thinking about how team members can work on tasks that require a quiet space free from distractions and disruptions. However, real life doesn't present such a clear-cut dichotomy in teamwork and many team leaders are involved in leading teams that are engaged on both process and

Table 5.1 Differences between process and project work

Process work	Project work
Predictable	Unpredictable
Involves repetition	Unique
Standardized	May be difficult to standardize
Takes place over a predictable time period	Takes place over an estimated time period
Maintains the status quo	Results in change

project work, and who also require quiet workspaces at times. This often means a balancing act between the needs of different people working on different types of work during the week.

To complicate matters further, there are different types of process and project work and they may involve individuals (or sub-teams) working independently, co-operatively or collaboratively. The differences between these types of work are outlined in Table 5.2 on the next page and different types of teamwork suggest different ways of organizing the working environment. For example, independent work does not require people to work in the same office although there are general benefits to working together in terms of information exchange, team development, etc. People who are working together on a collaborative project need to be able to spend time working together though this may take place in a virtual environment as well as face to face.

Managing routine work

Managing a team of people and ensuring that the work is completed on time and to the right standard is essential if the information or library service is to provide a good-quality service. Unless you are creating a new information and library service or department it is likely that you will be working in a context where the work of the department has been clearly identified and is well organized. Many supervisors plan the workload in their team by listing all the jobs that need to be carried out and then giving responsibility for different tasks to specific people. Routine work, which is carried out by all team members, e.g. staffing the help desk or enquiry point, is then organized by rota. In addition, arrangements need to be made for holidays or sick leave and for this reason many departments make sure that more than one person can carry out each task.

Planning

Sometimes team leaders are appointed to take on new projects or to improve the performance of an existing department or service. In this case the process of planning the work for the whole team will involve the following:

Table 5.2   Different types of teamwork

	Independent	Co-operative	Collaborative
Definition	Individuals work by themselves on their own tasks. They each have their own goal.	A task is divided into sections and individuals are responsible for their own piece of work. They each have their own goal.	The team works together on the task. They are working towards a shared goal.
Types of tasks	• Organizing room bookings • Acting as a contact person	• Producing a new website • Writing a report	• Producing a new website • Writing a report
Effective management patterns	• Individuals are briefed and deadlines agreed. • Individuals report back to team leader and/or team meetings	• Whole team is briefed and deadlines agreed. • Division of work is agreed. • Boundaries between tasks are clarified. • Individuals agree how they will communicate with each other and deal with critical or unexpected circumstances.	• Whole team is briefed and deadlines agreed. • Division of work is agreed. • Individuals discuss and agree how they will work with each other. • Future meeting dates are set for collaborative work to take place.

1 knowing what work there is to do now and in the near future
2 prioritizing tasks
3 identifying how much time it takes to complete a task
4 identifying the number of hours staff are available to work each week
5 identifying someone to complete the task
6 scheduling the tasks
7 delegating the task
8 providng appropriate workplace learning activities to ensure that team members can complete their tasks to the right standard
9 monitoring the whole process.

1   Knowing what work there is to do now and in the near future

• This involves listing all the tasks to be carried out. It may be helpful to organize the list into sections: daily, weekly, monthly, three-monthly, six-monthly and annual tasks.

- Identify the time spent on predictable activities, e.g. producing a monthly newsletter, and on activities where the workload is less easy to predict, e.g. special requests from senior managers, visits to the ILS by overseas visitors.
- It will involve using data collected as part of the day-to-day library operations, e.g. number of telephone and e-mail queries per day, number of readers coming to the library. If your ILS does not collect basic data on usage then it is important to start doing this. Statistical data are a vital information resource when arguing for a bigger budget or more staff, of if you are fighting against impending closure.
- Look at the ILS's strategic plan and talk with senior managers. This will help you to identify future changes that will have an impact on your workload.

2 Prioritizing tasks

- Identify the priority level of different tasks, whether they are high-, medium- or low-level priority.
- Investigate the low-priority tasks. Could they be deleted from the workload? What would happen if they were not completed?

3 Identifying how much time it takes to complete a task

- Experienced team members will be able to indicate how long it takes to complete a task.
- An equation is presented in the section on project management in this chapter and it may be used to estimate how long a particular job is likely to take.

4 Identifying the number of hours staff are available to work each week.

- This involves working out how many hours people are available to work each week.

5 Identifying someone to complete the tasks

- Identifying who will carry out each task during the working week is best carried out as a consultative process.
- This involves identifying the people who will be carrying out the task as part of their normal work role and taking into account their other tasks and commitments including holidays and workplace learning activities.
- It includes making sure that individuals have a good balance of different tasks during the day and ideally this will include a mixture of customer-service activities and also desk-based activities.

- It includes making sure that there is sufficient cover for busy periods, e.g. by operating a back-up system.
- It is important to identify times when people are not available, e.g. due to caring or other responsibilities.
- It includes giving people the opportunity to learn and develop new skills.

6 Scheduling the tasks

- Identify when the tasks need to be completed, e.g. by writing them on a wall calendar or in a desk diary.
- Charts are often used to schedule tasks as shown in the example given in Figure 5.1.

Weekly work plan   **Week beginning 24 October**

Tasks	Times	Monday	Tuesday	Wednesday	Thursday	Friday
Help desk	9–11 a.m.	Chris	Sumona	Stef	Paul	Chris
	11 a.m.–1 p.m.	Paul	Chris	Sumona	Stef	Paul
	1–3 p.m.	Stef	Paul	Chris	Sumona	Stef
	3–5 p.m.	Sumona	Stef	Paul	Chris	Sumona
Back-up help desk	9–11 a.m.	Stef	Paul	Chris	Sumona	Stef
	11 a.m.–1 p.m.	Sumona	Stef	Paul	Chris	Sumona
	1–3 p.m.	Chris	Sumona	Stef	Paul	Chris
	3–5 p.m.	Paul	Chris	Sumona	Stef	Paul
Phone enquiries	9–11 a.m.	Paul	Chris	Sumona	Stef	Paul
	11 a.m.–1 p.m.	Stef	Paul	Chris	Sumona	Stef
	1–3 p.m.	Sumona	Stef	Paul	Chris	Sumona
	3–5 p.m.	Chris	Sumona	Stef	Paul	Chris
Tidy work tables, check computers, check printer paper	9 a.m. 10.30 a.m. 2.30 p.m. 4.45 p.m.	Paul	Chris	Sumona	Stef	Paul

If you are not scheduled to be working on customer service activities then you are expected to use this time for your individual areas of responsibilities.

Figure 5.1 Weekly work schedule

Another approach to scheduling tasks involves using project management software such as MS Project. This may be used to produce a Gantt chart which shows tasks mapped across time. This is discussed later in this chapter and an example Gantt chart is shown in Figure 5.2. One of the advantages of using project management software is that a copy of the chart can be e-mailed to all staff.

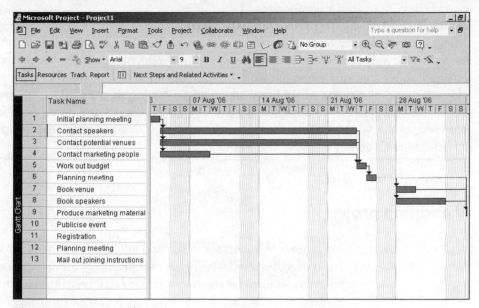

Figure 5.2 Gantt chart

7 Delegating the task

- This is covered later in this chapter.

8 Providing appropriate workplace learning activities to ensure that team members can complete their tasks to the right standard

- This is covered in Chapter 9.

9 Monitoring the whole process

- This involves identifying what is working well and the areas where there are problems.
- The most common methods of monitoring performance are by observation and hearing. Look out for areas where the work appears to be progressing smoothly and also areas where there are problems. Are backlogs developing? Listen to your team members and customers. Do they talk about some areas of their work positively? Are there constant grumbles about some tasks? Ask for feedback at team meetings.
- If you identify problem areas then bring the team together to work out a solution and improve current practices. You may find it useful to use the problem-solving technique introduced in Chapter 3.
- If you identify areas that are working really well then give praise.

Activity: Managing the routine work

The purpose of this activity is to enable you to review the way in which you plan the work of the team. You may find it useful to carry out this review with your team. Use the planning process outlined above and apply it to the work of your team. Identify areas where the work is well managed and also areas where the work could be managed more effectively or efficiently. Remember to praise staff for work that is done well and to discuss and agree ways in which the planning of the work could be improved. If necessary use the problem-solving technique introduced in Chapter 3.

Managing projects

Project work is now commonplace in ILS and information and library workers are regularly asked to get involved with projects as diverse as moving a library, merging two departments and introducing a new service or IT system. Many team leaders become involved in project work, e.g. you may be asked to manage a particular project or to become a member of a project team. In addition, your team members may also be members of a project team. Many of the ideas presented in this section of the chapter are developed in more detail in *Project Management* (Allan, 2004).

The traditional project management literature developed from work in industry and military projects and, as a result, offers an approach that is embedded in the scientific management field. These traditional approaches to project management tend to be concerned with splitting the project into its constituent parts and then managing and controlling the project process in a rather top-down authoritarian manner. While it is important in project management to approach the work in a reflective and logical manner, it is also important to appreciate the importance of people and the management of the relationships side of projects.

How does project work differ from the day-to-day work in an information or library department? The characteristics of projects include:

- definite start and end date
- unique and novel to the people involved in the project
- limiting factors, e.g. time, resources
- outcomes usually result in change
- single point of responsibility.

Examples of projects that fit these characteristics include the development of a new information website, the introduction of a portal, the merging of two libraries as a result of a company merger.

If you are involved in a new project then the first question to ask is 'How complex is the project?' Extremely complex projects require the use of project-management tools and techniques, whereas relatively simple projects can be managed using a sheet of A4. Factors to think about when assessing the complexity of a project include:

- Time issues
  - speed of project
  - speed of change
  - time allocated to work on project versus time for other duties, e.g. running the ILS
- Work issues
  - level of innovation
  - volumes of data
- People issues
  - size of team
  - levels of co-operation or collaboration
  - level of project – strategic or operations
  - working across different departments or organizations.

Why do projects go wrong? Newspapers thrive on stories of project failure and examples include projects that have gone over budget by millions or over time by years, e.g. many public-sector IT or building projects. Puleo (2002) identifies some of the more common pitfalls of project management:

- lack of project sponsor, e.g. by senior managers
- lack of a steering committee to achieve co-ordination and collaboration among people across organizations
- the wrong project manager, i.e. someone without the necessary project management, motivational, leadership and change-agent skills
- insufficient time for team members to carry out their project work
- lack of co-ordination between the project and everyday services.

Another common error is tackling a project that is so large and takes so long to implement that by the time the project is completed the product is redundant because the environment has changed, the user needs have changed, or the technology has moved on bringing with it new opportunities.

Project cycle

A standard approach to project management and one that helps to ensure that typical challenges are predicted and effectively managed is through the project cycle (see Figure 5.3). Each stage in this cycle is outlined below.

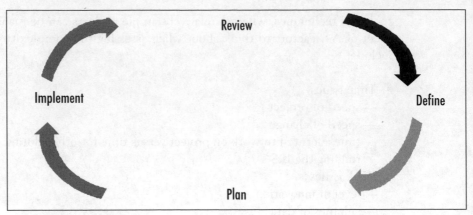

Figure 5.3 The project cycle

Defining the project

This involves the following steps:

- identify the basic aim of the project
- identify the project outcomes
- check that there is a match between the project and the organization's objectives
- identify the project team
- produce a project brief – one side of A4 that summarizes the proposed project
- identify milestones
- complete a cost–benefit analysis
- complete a risk analysis.

Project planning

This involves producing a project plan. For large and complex projects the plan is likely to expand on the project brief and should contain the following information:
- aims, outcomes and milestones
- a detailed list of the tasks that need to be completed and the time each task will take to be completed; this list may be presented as a Gantt chart (named after Henry Gantt). See Figure 5.2.
- network diagram, PERT chart (Pert stands for Programme Evaluation and Review Technique) or critical path diagram (terms tend to be used interchangeably). See Figure 5.4.
- week-by-week 'to do' list
- staffing requirements
- risk analysis
- contingency plans.

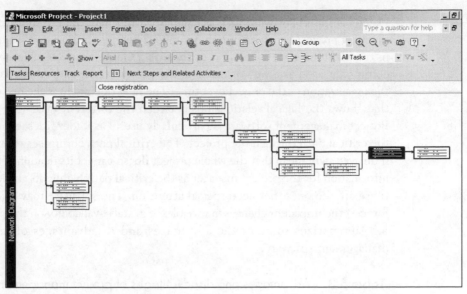

Figure 5.4 Network diagram/PERT Chart

Many organizations have their own template for project documentation so this is worth checking out before you produce your plans. If you are working on a very simple project then the project plan is likely to be a simple action plan.

An important aspect of the planning stage is to estimate how much time it will take to complete each task. A useful equation for calculating how much time it takes to complete a task is given below. This equation works out an average taking into account the best or most optimistic time, the worst or pessimistic time and the average time.

Estimate of time taken to complete a task = T (estimate)

$$T\text{ (estimate)} = \frac{T\text{ (optimistic)} + (4 \times T\text{ (average)}) + T\text{ (pessimistic)}}{6}$$

Worked example
Estimate the time taken to send out a mail shot of 500 letters.

Time (pessimistic)   = 12 hours
Time (average)   = 5 hours
Time (optimistic)   = 3 hours

$$\text{Time (estimate)} = \frac{[12 + (4 \times 5) + 3]}{6} = 5.8 \text{ hours}$$

Using computer software such as Excel or MS Project to help support the project planning process is now common practice. There are two important outputs used in the planning stages. The first of these is a Gantt chart (see Figure 5.2) that is commonly used as a way of enabling the project team and others to understand the organization of the project over time. The next document is the network diagram that shows the logical relationships between the different tasks (see Figure 5.4). Project management software is particularly useful as it identifies, generally in red, the critical path through the project. The critical path comprises those tasks that, if delayed, will mean that the whole project doesn't meet its deadline. This is useful information for the project manager as the critical path highlights the key tasks and these are the ones that need special attention. The software may also be used to forecast the impact of changes in variables, e.g. staff availability on the project. Table 5.3 summarizes some of the advantages and disadvantages of using project management software:

Table 5.3   Advantages and disadvantages of project management software

Advantages	Disadvantages
Provides a professional image	Time required to learn how to use software
Extensive range of reports	Data input can be time consuming
Big picture/detail views are possible	Garbage in garbage out (GIGO)
Send out daily/weekly 'to do' lists	
Impact of changes can be identified easily	

At the planning stage it is also worthwhile thinking about how you will communicate with the team and stakeholders throughout the project process. It is important to identify how you will find out about people issues, project progress, significant constraints, existing and potential problems, creep in project time (when tasks take longer than expected) and slack in project time (when tasks take less time than expected).

Implementation

This is when you actually start work on the project and this involves rolling out the plan including the communication strategy. The implementation process involves monitoring the following:

- staff motivation and morale
- progress on the project – tasks started and completed
- significant constraints
- existing problems
- potential problems

- creep in project time
- slack in project time.

The project management literature, e.g. Young (1999), tends to recommend setting up reporting systems to enable the project manager to keep control of progress in complex projects. In the types of projects that ILS staff are involved in monitoring the project is likely to be through a combination of 'walking around' and formal reporting systems. The latter may be as simple as asking every team member to e-mail the project manager with their progress once a week.

Project completion and review

The final stage of the project involves:

- production and dissemination of project reports
- checking to ensure that the project outcomes have been met
- dealing with loose ends, e.g. late invoices
- handing over the project to the team that will maintain it as part of the day-to-day services within the library
- project review
- celebration.

Complex projects will require detailed evaluations and reports, and a simple approach to reviewing small-scale projects involves asking team members and stakeholders to answer the following questions:

- What worked well?
- What could be improved?
- What did you learn?
- What will you do differently next time?

Although the traditional project management literature tends to focus on technical aspects of projects, it is the people side that is vital if the project is to be successful. (People issues are covered in Chapters 3 and 4.) Nowadays information and library workers may find themselves working in a variety of team situations ranging from small in-house teams through to multiskilled teams and collaborative teams made up of workers from a variety of professions and organizations. This topic is covered in more depth in Chapter 7.

Managing and working in a project team involves focusing on and working with individuals, the team and the task. As project manager or team leader you will need to know the individual team members and their strengths and weaknesses. You will be involved in action planning, giving and receiving information and feedback from team members, e.g. through e-mails or phone calls, and providing them with help and support as required. An important aspect of teamwork is motivation and you may be required to spend some time motivating and supporting staff. This is covered in Chapter 4.

Traditionally projects are managed through a series of teams (this is illustrated in Figure 5.5):

- Steering group. This group provides the overall strategic direction for the project and includes individuals who can champion the project throughout the organization, e.g. senior staff, directors.
- Management group. This group manages the operations of the project and resolves significant problems. It is likely to include the project manager and some key team members, and it may contain staff from other departments associated with the project, e.g. IT department.
- Project team. This is the operational team who carry out the work and resolve problems. They report to the management group.

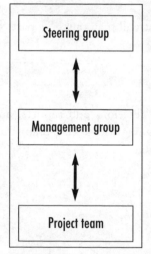

Figure 5.5
Project management structure

Sometimes the work of the management group and the project team may be merged, as shown in the example of the LawPort project (Miskin, 2006) in the company CMS Cameron McKenna. This project was managed through a steering group made up of the managing partner, directors of support departments and practice group managers, and the project team was multi-disciplinary and included representatives from all the support departments, professional support lawyers, key partners and key authors. In contrast, in small projects there may be only one team comprising the team leader and one or more team members, e.g. the LawBore project (Albion, 2005).

Another group of people who need to be considered comprises the stakeholders, e.g. all the staff within the organization, ILS staff not involved in the project, customers, suppliers, etc. As project manager it is worthwhile identifying the stakeholders and thinking about how you will communicate with them about the project. On very large projects, the project manager may want to set up a formal stakeholder panel or group as a means of establishing a two-way information flow with respect to the project.

Supervising staff

This section considers a number of topics that are essential to the successful supervision of staff, i.e. delegation, giving instructions, setting objectives, giving feedback, and monitoring and reviewing performance.

Delegation

Delegation involves entrusting another person with a task for which you remain ultimately responsible. Effective team leaders delegate specific tasks to team members: this involves giving responsibility for that particular task to another person. However, the team leader still remains accountable for the successful completion of the task. For example, a team leader could delegate responsibility for locking up the library at the end of the day to one of the team members but if they don't carry out the task correctly then the team leader is still accountable. In other words 'the buck stops here' with the team leader.

An advantage of delegation is that it enables other staff to develop their knowledge and skills, and they often find it motivating. In addition, delegation enables the team leader to move their focus to other aspects of the information and library service, e.g. the development of new products or services.

The delegation process involves the analysis and identification of task(s), identifying someone to delegate the task to, briefing them, providing appropriate workplace learning activities to make sure they can complete the task, monitoring and encouraging them, and reviewing and revising the process.

1 Analysis and identification of task(s)

- This involves identifying the tasks for delegation and considering whether they are routine or whether they require specialist skills or knowledge.
- It involves analysing what is required to complete the task.
- It involves identifying the risk involved in the delegation process going wrong.

2 Identifying the right person

- You need to think about your team members and their skills, knowledge, workload, development and progression plans.
- Many team leaders introduce tasks to be delegated in team meetings and give everyone the opportunity to discuss the task and the implications of it being delegated.
- Remember that you will still be accountable for the task – make sure that you pick the person who will deliver the goods.

3 Briefing

- When you brief someone to carry out the task you need to outline the objectives of the task, the resources available, the time scale, whether you want them to follow a detailed procedure or whether you are willing to give them an outline plan and let them carry out the task in their own style.

- You need to be very clear about what levels of authority they have in carrying out the task.
- You also need to outline what they should do if they have any problems.

4 Workplace learning

- Identify workplace learning, training or development required. You will need to identify whether this can be fulfilled by on-the-job or off-the-job learning activities. You also need to consider the costs of the development process in terms of time, resources and the expense involved in the team member not being available for other activities.

5 Monitoring systems

- You need to think about how often you will be monitoring the task.
- How will you monitor the work? Do you want to receive regular e-mails or verbal reports on progress? Will you have an open-door policy? Will you organize regular meetings? Will you monitor by walking about and observation?
- At what level will you monitor the task? Will you be involved in all correspondence, e.g. copied into all e-mails? Or is it sufficient to receive weekly or monthly progress reports on the task?

6 Monitoring and encouraging

- Do encourage team members to make their own decisions.
- Do move from hands-on to hands-off.
- Do ask for feedback.
- Do give the team member the opportunity to own the task.
- Don't doubt the delegate's ability.
- Don't take back the task.
- Don't interfere.

7 Support and encouragement

- Remember to give praise, support and encouragement.
- Let the team member own the task.
- If things go wrong then don't blame your colleague. Identify what can be learnt from the experience. Reflect on it (see Chapter 9).

8 Reviewing and revising

- Identify what went well.

- Identify what could be improved.
- Identify what has been learnt from the experience – by both the team member and yourself.
- Identify ways in which you could improve the delegation process.

Activity: Review your skills in delegation

The purpose of this activity is to review your skills in delegation. Choose a recent example of where you have delegated a task to a member of your team. Review this process using the following questions:

- What went well?
- What could be improved?
- What did I learn about my delegation skills?
- What should I do differently next time I delegate a task?

You may find it helpful to review this process with the team member as this will enable you to gain another perspective on your skills. You may find it helpful to discuss your findings with your manager or mentor, and to identify ways in which you could improve your delegation skills.

Giving instructions

It is a challenge to give clear instructions to another person so that they are able to follow them clearly. Most of us have experienced situations at work where someone gives an instruction and then exits the room leaving behind a very puzzled individual. Team leaders are likely to regularly give instructions to their team members and it is a skill worth developing.

The process of giving instructions involves the team leader identifying the following:

- aim of the activity
- reasons for the activity
- outcomes of the activity
- how to carry out the activity
- potential problems
- what the completed task will look like
- feedback required.

An example of this process is given in Figure 5.6.

Editing a mailing list database	
Aim of the activity	To remove duplicate records from the information department mailing list.
Reasons for the activity	Duplicate records result in a waste of money and also sending out duplicate letters is bad for the image of the service.
Outcomes of the activity	A database with no duplicate records; more professional mailouts; no complaints arising from the receipt of duplicates.
How to carry out the activity	Print out the database in alphabetical order by named person. Work through printout and cross out duplicate records. Go into the database and delete the duplicate records.
Potential problems	Duplicates arising from people being entered on database with alternative names or spelling of names – check for these by working through a printout in organization order.
What the completed task will look like	When printed out the database should contain no duplicates.
Feedback required	Once the task is completed provide an up-to-date printout to the team leader.

Figure 5.6 Giving instructions

Setting objectives

Most team leaders will be involved in setting and agreeing objectives with their team members. A common approach to setting objectives is to use what is known as the SMART approach where SMART stands for Specific, Measurable, Achievable, Relevant and Time-based.

Specific in the context of setting objectives means that it is an observable action or result that is also linked with a number, e.g. the number of times a task needs to be completed; the production of a specific product, e.g. report or website; the completion of a set piece of work, e.g. cataloguing all new books within two working days of their arrival in the ILS. An example of a specific objective is to check that the printers have sufficient paper three times a day.

Measurable means that the objective can be measured, e.g. if someone is checking the printers three times a day then this can be measured by someone monitoring the member of staff, or the person checking the printers may sign a work schedule each time they have carried out the activity. This work schedule then provides a record of the completed objectives.

The set objectives must be achievable and this involves making sure that the team member has the appropriate level of knowledge and skills to carry out the objective. It also means that it is achievable given the amount of time and energy available for carrying out the objective. There is a real skill in setting achievable objectives and ideally they will not be too easy or simple but will provide a challenge that then becomes motivating.

SMART objectives are relevant and this means that they will make a positive impact on customers and services, the ILS and the organization. Setting objectives that are relevant are motivating as team members appreciate their importance to the daily work of the team and department.

Time-based means that within the SMART objective there is an indication of time. For example the objective may need to be completed by a specific date or an individual must spend a set amount of time on the objective each day, week or month.

Examples of SMART objectives include:

- I will check the printers in the library to make sure that they are working properly and that they are fully loaded with paper three times a day (Monday to Friday).
- I will produce a draft copy of the new ILS newsletter by the 14 January and it will be two sides of A4 long.
- I will check the ILS website for broken web-links once a month.

The advantages of SMART objectives are that they are very clear and help communications between the team leader and individual team members. Their clarity helps to reduce areas for potential disagreements. Ideally objectives will be discussed and jointly agreed between the team leader and members as this helps them to be owned by all parties.

The following examples (see Figures 5.7 and 5.8) show two slightly different approaches that may be used for agreeing a SMART objective with a team member.

Activity: Review your skills in giving instructions

The purpose of this activity is to review your skills in giving instructions. Choose a recent example of where you have given instructions to a member of your team. Review this process asking the following questions:

- What went well?
- What could be improved?
- What did I learn about my ability to give instructions?
- What should I do differently next time I give instructions?

You may find it helpful to review this process with the team member, as this will enable you to gain another perspective on your skills. You may find it helpful to discuss your findings with your manager or mentor, and to identify ways in which you could improve your ability to give instructions.

1 **What is the SMART objective?**
Remember to be Specific, Measurable, Achievable, Relevant and Time-based.

2 **What resources will you need to do your activity?**
Do you need any special information resources or equipment?

3 **What support will you need?**
Will it be easier if you do it with another team member? Do you need support from the team leader? Do you need support from a mentor?

4 **When will you have completed your task or how often will you do it?**
Set a specific date and time or set yourself a target, e.g. 15 minutes every day.

5 **Who will check your progress and review your activity with you?**
How will your progress on the activity be monitored and reviewed?

Figure 5.7 Sample personal action plan 1

1 **What will you do?   Choose a particular task or activity.**
Remember to ensure that it is Specific, Measurable, Achievable, Relevant and Time-based.

2 **When will you do it?**

3 **Where will you do it?**

4 **Will you be working by yourself or with someone else? If you are working with someone else then have you obtained their support?**

5 **What will you see, hear and feel when you have achieved your objective?**

6 **Is there anything that will stop you from doing it? How can you prevent this happening?**

7 **How will you reward yourself when you have completed your task/activity?**

Figure 5.8 Sample personal action plan 2

Giving feedback

Feedback is an important source of learning and it is an essential part of working with others. Ideally feedback takes place at the time of the event or as soon as possible afterwards. Feedback helps to produce improved performance and it is essential to maintain continuous improvement. One way of viewing feedback is as a gift. How do we package this gift? How have we thought about it, selected it and wrapped it up? People have different tolerances for feedback and one useful way of thinking about this is through the metaphor of buckets, tumblers or thimbles:

- Buckets. Some people are ready and willing to receive feedback and may even seek it out. They are confident and want to develop. Beware of people who are like buckets with holes as here nothing changes and the feedback goes through and out of the bucket without even touching the sides!
- Tumblers. Some people are able to take in a small amount of feedback and are likely to respond to it.
- Thimbles. People who are like thimbles are likely to lack confidence and feel insecure. They may doubt their ability to improve and are overwhelmed if they think that they are not doing a good job. These people may be able to receive only a very small amount of feedback at any time.

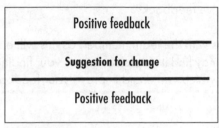

Figure 5.9
The feedback sandwich

A common approach to packaging the feedback is to use the sandwich method which involves presenting positive feedback, then a suggestion for change followed by another positive statement. This is illustrated in Figure 5.9. A key point about the sandwich approach is that each part of the sandwich needs to be about the same size. An over-thick centre can cause indigestion!

Another approach to giving feedback is illustrated in Figure 5.10. This involves asking the member of staff for their feedback on their performance, then asking them how it could be improved, and finally providing positive feedback. This approach helps the team member to own the feedback and their own continuous improvement at work.

Ask a team member how they thought they have performed
Ask them for a suggestion for improvement
The team leader provides positive feedback

Figure 5.10
The learner's feedback sandwich

The following list provides guidance on giving feedback:

- Be clear about the purpose of giving feedback. What do you want to achieve?
- Start with the positive.
- Be specific.
- Refer to a behaviour that can be changed.
- Offer alternatives.
- Be descriptive rather than evaluative.
- Take ownership of feedback by using 'I' statements such as 'I have noticed . . .'.
- Leave the recipient with a choice.

- Give the feedback as soon as possible after the event.
- Think about what the feedback says about you!

Activity: Review your feedback skills

The purpose of this activity is to review your feedback skills. Choose a recent example of where you have given feedback to a member of your team. Review this process using the following questions:

- What went well?
- What could be improved?
- What did I learn about my feedback skills?
- What should I do differently next time I give feedback?

You may find it helpful to review this process with the team member, as this will enable you to gain another perspective on your skills. You may find it helpful to discuss your findings with your manager or mentor, and to identify ways in which you could improve your feedback skills.

Monitoring and reviewing performance

As team leader you need to monitor the work of your team and to ensure that the work is completed to the required standard. In addition, you need to be aware of blockages to work being completed, tasks that are taking longer to complete than expected (this is called slippage) and tasks that are completed ahead of time. Reiss (2000) identifies two approaches to monitoring progress:

- Monitoring by walking around. Walk around the department, talk with team members, observe what is happening and ask for feedback when you think it is appropriate. One of the advantages of this approach is that sometimes small problems or potential problems can be identified extremely early and a solution can be worked out with the team involved in that part of the project. It also enables you to be visible to your team and accessible so that individuals may raise their queries or concerns with you.
- Setting up a reporting system. You ask other people to measure progress and report back to you at regular intervals. This may involve individual team members giving you regular verbal reports or e-mails. Problems and potential problems may then be identified and addressed through regular meetings or, if they are relatively small, by e-mail or phone conversations.

The majority of team leaders and managers use a mixture of these two methods depending on their context and the nature of the work. Many team leaders hold brief meetings, e.g. at the start of the day, as a means of assessing where staff are with their individual tasks and then change the work schedule in response to the current situation. In well established teams with experienced staff the team may be performing effectively and to the right standards and, in this situation, little formal monitoring of the work may need to take place. However, in new and developing teams it is essential that the team leader regularly monitors the work to ensure that it is carried out to the correct standards.

In teams involving different people who are perhaps working on different sites then a simple process such as everyone e-mailing the team leader with information about the state of all the tasks at set times each week will give the manager the necessary information. The pro-forma in Figure 5.11 may be used for generating reports from team members.

Weekly progress report from _____			
Task number and name	Start date	End date	Current status/comments
Major concerns/issues			
Signature: Date:			

Figure 5.11 Weekly progress report

Managing staff performance

When you are monitoring the work of the team you may recognize that individual members of staff are not performing their work to the appropriate standards. There are a number of ways of tackling this issue:

- Talk with the individual member of staff about their performance and see if you can identify the underlying issue. It may be that they are unaware of the required standards or that they require additional training. If you are able to identify a simple solution then agree an action plan and review their work after one or two weeks. You may find some of the assertiveness techniques covered in Chapter 3 helpful as a means of tackling this type of situation.
- If an informal discussion does not help to resolve the situation then meet with the member of staff again and discuss the issue with them. Explain that it is a serious issue and that it needs to be resolved. You both need to identify a solution, then agree an action plan and review their work after one or two weeks. You may find some of the assertiveness techniques covered in Chapter 3 helpful as a means of tackling this type of situation.

- If the situation is not resolved at this stage then my advice is to talk with your human resources department (see Chapter 8) and use your organization's policies and procedures to tackle the issue in a more formal manner.

Managing blockages

Blockages occur for a wide range of reasons, e.g. someone may be waiting for a vital piece of information before they can start their task; a training event may be cancelled meaning that staff don't have the appropriate skills for the task; there may be a misunderstanding about what is required and team members may have 'forgotten' the task or relegated it low in their personal priorities. Whatever the reason for the blockage it is up to the team leader to identify the cause of the blockage and to come up with an acceptable solution that enables the staff to get on with their work. This may involve the problem-solving process outlined in Chapter 3.

Managing slippage

Slippage occurs when it takes longer than anticipated to complete particular tasks and so it becomes impossible to adhere to the team's work schedule. Once the team leader or manager has identified that the schedule is slipping and different tasks may not be completed on time then there are a number of different common responses:

- **Obtain additional resources**. This might mean obtaining more people to work on the activity or project. While this may appear to be an attractive option common experience in IT projects suggests that simply adding more staff to the task may delay the work even further! The new people will need time to be trained and work up-to-speed with the team's activities or project and so may take time away from the current team. Carefully introducing a small number of additional people does sometimes produce benefits and this is often when they are given very specific tasks to complete and ones with which they are very familiar.
- **Ask people to work harder or to work longer hours**. In the short term this strategy can work. If there is money available in the budget then paying some additional overtime can pay dividends. However, if this is used as a long-term solution it can demotivate staff and lead to stress, burn out and an increase in sick leave or staff turnover.
- **Review the work and reduce its scope**. Reviewing the scope of the work and either cutting out some of the outcomes or postponing them until later can sometimes deal with slippage. Improving the flow of work or organizing it in a different manner may also achieve it.

- **Accept the slippage**. Sometimes this is the most sensible course of action and the team leader needs to think through their work schedule and update it to take into account the reality of the situation.

Quality

The quality of the work must be monitored to ensure that you meet the required standards. Ideally you will have information about the quality criteria and also how these will be checked. All team members need to be responsible for monitoring quality so they need to be pro-active and start off their quality processes and procedures from the start of work on the task. They also need to report their findings to the team leader on a regular basis. This will enable appropriate adjustments to be made to the working practices of the team extremely quickly.

Reviewing the work of the team

It is important to review the work of the team. This may involve reviewing all the work carried out by the team, a particular aspect of the work such as a new service, the way in which the work is managed, or the communication processes within the team.

When and how do you review teamwork? The process of identifying and spending some time reviewing teamwork is likely to be repaid as the team learns to become reflective and learn from their successes and weaknesses. Teamwork may be reviewed regularly, e.g. every month or every three months, and this is dealt with during regular team meetings. The following questions may be used as prompts for reviewing teamwork:

- Did we achieve our objectives?
- Did we produce work to the required standards?
- What are our main successes/failures?
- In what areas did we not achieve our objectives?
- Did working as a team help or hinder the achievement of our objectives?
- Did we produce better/worse work as a result of working in the team?
- How effective was the team in working together?
- Did the team help and support individuals in their work?
- What were the main strengths/weaknesses of teamwork?
- How could we improve our outcomes?
- How could we improve teamworking?
- What are the main learning points for next time?

One technique that I have used is to ask appropriate people, e.g. team members and other stakeholders, four questions:

- What did we achieve?
- What went well?
- What did we learn?
- What should we do differently if we were to repeat the work?

A simple way of obtaining this information is to divide a piece of flipchart paper, a whiteboard or even a sheet of A4 paper into four and designate a space for each of the questions, as illustrated in Figure 5.12. Individuals or small groups can then complete the questions and their answers can be included in the team leader's report if they need to report on their work to a senior manager, or the responses may be used by the team and its leader to improve future performance.

Activity: Review the work of your team

The purpose of this activity is to review the work of your team. Identify time in your next team meeting for this activity. Review the work of your team using Figure 5.12. You may find it helpful to write this grid on a piece of flipchart paper so that you and your team complete the grid together. At the end of the activity produce an action plan to tackle one or two issues that arose during the process. Thank your team members for their work on this activity. You may find it helpful to discuss your findings with your manager or mentor, and to identify ways in which you could improve your delegation skills. This activity could be repeated at three-monthly intervals.

What did we achieve?	What went well?
What did we learn?	What should we do differently if we were to repeat the work?

Figure 5.12 Simple team review process

Summary

The aim of this chapter is to provide guidance on managing both routine and project work in an ILS, and organizing and providing a professional work environment for both readers and staff. This chapter emphasizes the importance of planning and organizing both routine and project work. In addition it considers the people side with topics such as delegating tasks, giving instructions, giving feedback, setting goals and monitoring and reviewing performance.

References

Albion, E. (2005) It's Alive! The Birth of LawBore and the Indispensability of the Law Librarian, *Legal Information Management*, 5 (4), 211–14.

Allan, B. (2004) *Project Management: tools and techniques for today's ILS professional*, London, Facet Publishing.

Miskin, C. (2006) The BIALL/Lexis Nexis Awards for Excellence, *Legal Information Management*, 6 (2), 76–89.

Puleo, L. (2002) Some of the More Common Pitfalls of Project Management, *Accounting Today*, www.electronicaccount.com/AccountingToday/.

Reiss, G. (2000) *Project Management Demystified*, 2nd edn, London, Spon Press.

Young, T. L. (1999) *The Handbook of Project Management*, London, Kogan Page.

6 Communication skills

Introduction

The aim of this chapter is to provide an outline of the communication skills required by team leaders and supervisors. Excellent communication skills are at the heart of teamworking and they involve people in thinking about the person to whom they are communicating, what they want to communicate, and the most effective means of getting their message across. This chapter considers the following topics: communications in organizations, communicating with the team, e.g. briefing teams and individuals, leading meetings, listening and presentation skills and using virtual communication tools.

Communications in organizations

It is traditional to classify the communications processes in organizations into formal and informal systems.

Formal communications

Formal communication systems are those set up by the organization to ensure that the organization and its staff work towards their goals in an efficient and effective manner. Formal communication processes include:

- Written communications:
  — formal letters, minutes of meetings and memos
  — annual reports
  — procedure manuals.
- Verbal communications:
  — manager's briefings
  — formal meetings.

Large organizations often have a department, frequently the marketing or communications department, that is concerned with internal as well as external communications. Individual managers and team leaders may be provided with guidance about the communication standards within their organization and department. However, the communications processes within a department or team are the responsibility of the managers, team leaders or supervisors. In small organizations individual managers will take much greater responsibility for all communication processes including external communications relevant to their department.

Informal communications

Informal communications include written communications such as notes, birthday cards and e-mails, and a whole range of activities such as gossip, discussions over lunch or in the pub and informal meetings over a photocopier. An important difference between formal and informal communications is that while the management of an organization has some control over the formal communication processes they have little control over the informal ones. Informal networks exist where people communicate outside the formal channels and they are an important source of information as well as misinformation!

Methods of communication

Communications, both within the organization and external communications, may take place in written or verbal forms. A wide range of written communications may be used in organizations, e.g. letters, reports, memos, e-mail, notices, newsletters, agenda and minutes of meetings. As team leader it is worthwhile thinking which of these methods are appropriate within your team. Some of them will be supported by visual images, e.g. charts and graphs, pictures and photographs, symbols, flowcharts, maps and plans, which help to summarize and simplify complicated information. Visual images help to give impact to your message and they tend to be more memorable than simple text.

Verbal communications include those taking place over the telephone and in meetings (one-to-one or group). As team leader, it is worthwhile considering when it is more appropriate to talk with another person rather than communicate via e-mail, and also whether the conversation should be held in private or as part of a group meeting.

Different types of information are communicated within an organization, including:

- strategic information, e.g. about long-term goals and objectives
- speculative or hypothetical information, e.g. possible future scenarios or implications arising from potential decisions
- management and financial information, e.g. sales, salaries, budgets
- human resource/personnel information, e.g. health and safety, equal opportunities, new employment legislation
- operational information, e.g. specific information about systems or products
- cultural or attitudinal information, e.g. relating to values of an organization.

There are different preferred ways of communicating this information within an organization and this is illustrated in Table 6.1.

Table 6.1 Communicating different types of information
Note: adapted from the work of Leigh and Walters, 1998.

Information	Audience	Most appropriate media
Strategic information	Senior management; managers and team leaders	Formal report or presentation; newsletter or presentation
Speculative or hypothetical information	Senior management; managers and team leaders	Formal report or consultative presentation; scenario-planning event; presentation with opportunity for extended discussion
Management and financial information	Senior management; managers and team leaders	Formal report perhaps supported by presentation; formal newsletter or presentation; e-mail with attached information
Human resource/personnel information	Senior management; managers and team leaders; general workforce	Formal report perhaps supported by presentation; formal newsletter; e-mail with attached information
Operational information	Managers and team leaders; general workforce	Management summary report; newsletter, notice, manual, memo; e-mail with attached information
Cultural or attitudinal information	Senior management; managers and team leaders; general workforce	Face-to-face presentation with discussion

Communicating with the team

As team leader the main focus of your communication processes will be with your team. A useful starting point is to consider the relative importance of body language, the tone of your communications, and the actual words used in communicating with others. This is covered in Chapter 3.

Team leaders are often required to convince or motivate individuals to accept a particular idea or to follow a new work procedure. A particularly useful model of communication comes from the body of knowledge with the unfortunate name of neurolinguistic programming (NLP). This model provides a framework for thinking about how to communicate with individuals and the whole team. It identifies two aspects of the communication process: individual preferences for taking in information; and the timescale of the process. This model recognizes that individuals prefer to take in information in a number of different ways, e.g. visual (seeing images or reading text), auditory, kinaesthetic or actually doing something, and is summarized in Table 6.2. The implications for team leaders are that when communicating with the team as a whole you need to use a variety of methods.

Table 6.2 Convincer patterns – information channels
Note: adapted from Charvet (1997)

Name	Overview
Visual	• **Seeing images**. These people will need to see the new information, e.g. in a diagram, metaphor, or visual image built up from words. • **Reading text**. These people prefer to read about something in an e-mail, report or briefing document.
Audio	These people need to hear the situation described to them. They often need to spend a lot of time talking things through, perhaps going over the same ground a number of times.
Kinaesthetic	These people actually need to experience the situation, i.e. have experience of doing something or remember an experience when they did it.

In addition to the methods of presenting information you also need to think about the timing because different people prefer exposure to new ideas and decisions in different ways. A minority of people are comfortable with making decisions and taking on board new ideas if they experience them once and this is due to an automatic convincer. In contrast, the majority of people prefer to experience the new idea a number of times, typically three times, and this is the reason why presentations and news programmes are commonly structured around an introduction, main content and summary, giving the presenter the opportunity to mention the important items three times. This explains the training adage 'Tell them what you are going to tell them, tell them, and then tell them what you have told them.' Other people need a period of time, e.g. one or two weeks, to accept new ideas or ways of working and, finally, some people have a 'never' convincer and will not accept new approaches to working. Fortunately, the latter are relatively small in number. The time aspects of the convincer model are summarized in Table 6.3.

I have found this model helpful in both thinking through and planning team communications, and also in identifying where a communication process has failed. It is important to be aware that individual convincer preferences are context dependent and may vary over time. This means that an individual's preference is likely to be different in the workplace to home, and it may be different when they are working on a familiar help desk to when they are taking part in a challenging training course. The power of this model is illustrated in Case studies 6.1 and 6.2.

Case study 6.1   Developing a team leader's communication skills

Chris, an information officer working for a law company, complained that his team of six were really bad at following instructions and 'resisted' new ideas and practices. When

Table 6.3   Convincer patterns – timing
Note: adapted from Charvet (1997)

Timing	Characteristics
Automatic	These people will base their judgements and make decisions on very small amounts of information. They will leap to conclusions without being bothered about having to wait. They often find it hard to change their minds
Number of examples	These people need to see, hear or do things a number of times before they are convinced. The majority of people with this pattern need three briefings.
Over time	These people need time (a few days or weeks) before they accept and are convinced by new ideas or practices.
Never	These people are never really convinced and need to re-evaluate issues and ideas time and time again. In discussions they may want to return to an earlier point all over again.

asked how he communicated with his team he said that they had a team meeting twice a year and in-between times he sent e-mails. Further discussion uncovered that he would send one e-mail out as a means of communicating anything from information about a new acquisition to introducing a new working procedure.

Chris was introduced to the convincer model of communications and, as a result, expanded his repertoire of communication tools. He changed his communication style to include more regular meetings where he occasionally used PowerPoint presentations; he sent out regular e-mails; and he asked a team member to introduce A4 size posters to summarize the new working procedure. The feedback he obtained from this change was extremely positive and he reported that his team had become much more hard working and less resistant to change. He did complain that the new communication methods took up more time.

Case study 6.2   A summer move
A number of years ago I led a team that managed a summer moving project in a university ILS department. One of the team members had a convincer pattern of the 'never' variety. Throughout the project he constantly pointed out that we would never meet our deadlines or targets. We did achieve them. The day after the end of the move I met him in the car park and mentioned how good it was that we had met our goals. He responded by saying: 'Of course it was a fluke and we were just lucky. We will never be able to achieve that result a second time.' Words failed me!

For team leaders it is worthwhile being conscious of this pattern of taking on board new ideas. If you are working with someone who will never be convinced about something then it is a waste of time to put huge amounts of effort into convincing them. As with all convincers each convincer brings with it advantages and disadvantages.

Apparently many copy-editors and also health and safety inspectors have a 'never' convincer: this means they persistently look for errors or problems and are not easily satisfied by reassurances from others.

Working and communicating with a team is relatively simple because if you cover all the information channels and timings identified in Tables 6.2 and 6.3, then you will meet the convincer preferences of all team members. How do you identify individual convincer patterns? If you want to find out how someone is convinced about something then the simple question 'What will convince you . . .?' will produce the information you need to inform your communication strategy with that person.

Finally, team leaders will tend to plan their communications processes based on their own convincer preferences so someone whose preferences are auditory and automatic will expect team members to be convinced about something if they mention it once to them. Once we become aware of our own preferences then we can expand our communications repertoire to cover all the common preferences explored above. This will help us to become more effective as team leaders.

Activity: Planning a communication process

The next time you need to communicate a new service or change in working practices to your customers then use the convincer model to identify whether or not you have covered all the necessary information channels and the different time patterns people have. Use the following list (or Tables 6.2 and 6.3) to identify any gaps in your strategy and then work out how to fill these gaps.

Have you covered the following information channels and time patterns?

- visual – seeing images
- visual – reading text
- audio
- kinaesthetic
- number of examples, e.g. three
- over time.

The convincer model of communications is useful in terms of planning team briefings. Team leaders are often required to brief teams, e.g. about changes in the day-to-day routine, new projects or activities within the organization. One useful outline for organizing a briefing meeting is given below:

1 Welcome everyone and introduce the meeting.
2 Explain why you are holding the meeting, e.g. who has asked you to brief staff, why the topic of the meeting is a current issue.
3 Explain the new situation. Provide answers to the following questions: who, why, what, when, how.

4 Explain how it will affect your team and department.
5 Provide time for questions and answers.
6 End the meeting.
7 Follow up the meeting by sending out an e-mail that summarizes the situation and answers any questions that you were unable to answer at the time.

When you are briefing the team it is useful to consider how you may use the ideas presented in the previous section. This involves making sure that you provide information in a variety of ways, e.g. visual by PowerPoint presentation and handouts; auditory by providing a verbal explanation and a question-and-answer session; kinaesthetic by providing opportunities to work with a new system. In addition you need to repeat your message a number of times, ideally three times.

Leading successful meetings

Many people feel that time spent in meetings is unproductive and that most meetings are a waste of time, yet meetings are essential to good management. As a team leader it is important to develop skills in leading effective meetings and the key to this is detailed planning.

Planning a meeting

When you are setting up a meeting it is worthwhile considering the following questions:

- What is the purpose of the meeting?
- What decisions need to be made at the meeting?
- Who needs to attend the meeting?
- Do they need to attend the whole meeting?
- What is the most convenient time to hold the meeting?
- Where should the meeting be held?
- How will people who are unable to attend the meeting be updated on the discussions and outcomes of the meeting?

The answers to these questions will help inform your planning process. It is considered good practice to produce and circulate an agenda for the meeting beforehand as this enables participants to think about the issues that will be discussed. Figure 6.1 on the next page shows a sample e-mail sent out to advertise a forthcoming meeting.

Many organizations have their own standard ways of writing and formatting the minutes of meetings. If you are working in an organization of this kind then it is worthwhile finding out about the desired standards, e.g. by attending a relevant staff training event. If your organization doesn't have a set standard approach to

From: Sam Jones
To: All members of the Information Service
Subject: Team meeting 12 January

Hello everyone,
This is to remind you that our next departmental team meeting is on Friday 12 January at 2 pm in the Training room. The meeting should last no longer than an hour.

Items on the agenda include: ICT training programme; new handouts; new rota. I enclose the notes from our last meeting.

See you on Friday (if not before!).

Sam

Figure 6.1 E-mail advertising a meeting

Information Services team. Team meeting 12 January 2007

Present: Sam Jones, Mohammed Abosag, Jane Smith, Jasmine Farrow
Absent: Janice Kirby (annual leave)

1 Notes of last meeting – agreed as correct
2 Matters arising
    2.1 New opening hours – these have been implemented.
    2.2 Customers appear to like the late evening on Thursday. No problems noted.
    2.3 Induction day for new staff – this worked well. New staff were positive about the library induction session. All the new staff have made at least one visit to the library.
3 ICT training programme. Jane and Mohammed have rewritten the programme and produced some new activities. It was agreed to pilot the programme to Information Services staff asap. Action: Jane to organize a pilot before the end of February.
4 New handouts – Jasmine produced draft new handouts on information searching. They look excellent. Action: all colleagues to read through handouts and give feedback to Jasmine by 15 February.
5 New rota – Sam outlined reasons for a new rota. Janice had sent a message saying that she was worried about the possibility of working on Thursday evening owing to her childcare commitments. Sam said that individual circumstances would be taken into account in the new rota. Action: Sam to e-mail all Information staff on Monday and ask them to let her know their working time preferences by 20 January.
6 Date of next meeting – 15 February.

Figure 6.2 Notes from a meeting

recording meetings it is a good idea to keep a record of the meeting. Figure 6.2 shows a simple approach to keeping notes of a meeting.

Why do so many meetings go wrong? Meetings go wrong for two main reasons: errors in planning the meeting and weaknesses in chairing the meeting. The following examples outline some of the errors that take place in planning meetings. First, the wrong people may be attending the meeting and this can result in people becoming bored because they don't have anything to contribute; it may be difficult to make decisions because the right people aren't present; and people who have not been invited may feel rejected and not accept the outcomes of the meeting. Second, some aspects of the meeting may have been badly planned. The timing might be wrong; relevant papers may not have been circulated before the meeting; or too much information is given to members. The venue might be wrong too, e.g. it might be too hot or too cold, cramped and stuffy, have uncomfortable furniture or the meeting may be held in a formal boardroom, which some people find intimidating. The history of the room has an impact on the meeting too. For example, I previously worked in a university where one room was regularly used by senior managers to brief staff with bad news. As a result, staff associated this room with bad news and so whenever a meeting was held there they would often switch into defensive positions and not be positive or open-minded about new ideas. I soon learnt never to organize a meeting in this room!

Chairing a meeting

A weak or inexperienced chair may make a number of mistakes:

- They may start the meeting either late or early and this is likely to irritate some people.
- They may not start with introductions and this can make for an uncomfortable start when people don't know each other.
- A weak chair is often unclear about the purpose of the meeting and doesn't focus on decisions and actions. They are likely not to control the discussion and so the meeting will inevitably drift into topics not on the agenda or a level of detail that is not needed.
- Some weak chairs will let the meeting spend time talking about topics over which they have no influence, i.e. that are beyond the responsibility of the meeting.
- Poor meetings may be dominated by one or two people and the chair doesn't bring in quieter members.
- Badly managed meetings may overrun their time, or finish early but without making key decisions, and there may be no record of decisions or actions.

The chairperson has a pivotal role in the success or failure of any meeting. Chairing a meeting can be a daunting prospect if you are unused to it. Effective chairpersons prepare an agenda and consider issues such as people's responses to items on the agenda in working out the order of topics. They select the meeting room and make sure that the furniture is organized with a view to creating the right atmosphere. Finally, they invite the people likely to contribute most and use firm but subtle group control. Below are some guidelines that can be used to ensure that you lead effective meetings.

Guidelines for effective meetings

1 Be clear about the objectives of the meeting:
   - Why are you having the meeting?
   - What decisions need to be made at the meeting?
2 Prepare the agenda:
   - The agenda should reflect the objectives of the meeting.
   - It should have a definite start and finish time.
   - Check the order of the agenda. Don't start or end with highly emotive topics.
   - Check the agenda to see if there are items on it that could be dealt with by other means, e.g. e-mail, one-to-one discussions.
3 Make sure the right people attend the meeting:
   - Invite the people who have a genuine contribution to make to the discussions.
   - Invite people who have specialist information that is relevant to the decisions that are to be made.
   - Invite people who are stakeholders, i.e. they have an investment in the topics under consideration and need to be part of the decision-making process.
4 Plan the arrangements for the meeting:
   - Select an appropriate time for the meeting.
   - Select an appropriate room.
   - Check the layout of the room. Make sure that everyone will be comfortable and able to see and hear each other.
   - Consider refreshments. Will you need to organize refreshments for the meeting?
   - Ask someone to take notes of the meeting.
5 The actual meeting:
   - Arrive early with the correct paperwork.
   - Welcome everyone as they arrive.
   - If people don't know each other then make introductions.
   - Welcome new members of staff.
   - Keep to the agenda.
   - Summarize at the end of each agenda item.
   - Control problem members.
   - Ensure everyone present contributes.

- At the end of the meeting, thank everyone for attending and for their contributions.
6 After the meeting:
  - Make sure that notes of the meeting are written up and circulated to team members.
  - Make sure that actions decided at the meeting take place.

Activity: How well do you chair meetings?

The aim of this activity is to enable you to reflect on your ability to chair meetings. Look at Figure 6.3 and consider the list of positive behaviours and score yourself (0 = never, 10 = always). Alternatively, you may ask a colleague to complete the score sheet for you. Once you have obtained the results from the checklist then reflect on them. Identify the areas where you score highly. Identify areas for improvement. You may like to use this information to consider how you will improve the quality of the next meeting that you chair.

Do you . . .	Never . . . . . . always
make sure that you have prepared and circulated the right documents?	0 1 2 3 4 5 6 7 8 9 10
think through the different agenda items and how individuals might respond to them?	0 1 2 3 4 5 6 7 8 9 10
keep to time?	0 1 2 3 4 5 6 7 8 9 10
keep the discussions on topic?	0 1 2 3 4 5 6 7 8 9 10
ask quiet team members for their thoughts?	0 1 2 3 4 5 6 7 8 9 10
manage dominant members?	0 1 2 3 4 5 6 7 8 9 10
deal with difficult topics in a sensitive manner?	0 1 2 3 4 5 6 7 8 9 10
give others the chance to speak?	0 1 2 3 4 5 6 7 8 9 10
explain your reasons for disagreement?	0 1 2 3 4 5 6 7 8 9 10
listen to the viewpoints of others even when you disagree with them?	0 1 2 3 4 5 6 7 8 9 10
prevent the meeting from becoming bogged down in too much detail?	0 1 2 3 4 5 6 7 8 9 10
prevent general moaning sessions?	0 1 2 3 4 5 6 7 8 9 10
follow up if you agree to take action?	0 1 2 3 4 5 6 7 8 9 10
ensure that the notes from the meeting are written up and circulated within a reasonable time period?	0 1 2 3 4 5 6 7 8 9 10

Figure 6.3   How well do you chair meetings?

Listening skills

A crucial part of all communication processes involves listening to the other person. Active listening involves listening with your whole body and whole brain. Developing your listening skills improves performance in the following areas:

- obtaining information
- learning people's opinions
- exploring people's feelings and attitudes
- clarifying a misunderstanding
- assessing or appraising
- picking up small and perhaps very significant points of view
- demonstrating that you are actively involved and interested.

Active listening involves making sure that your whole attention is on the other person and that you are listening to both the words they say and also noticing their body language. Body language provides valuable information about the other person's emotions. There are a number of different ways in which you can demonstrate that you are actively listening to the other person as illustrated in the following:

- Reflecting   'Let me see if I've got your point . . .'
- Supporting   'Yes, that's a good idea . . .'
    'And then?'
- Constructing   'Would it help if we . . . ?'
    'What would you like to happen . . . ?'
- Clarifying   'Are you saying that . . . ?'
- Interpreting   'So you seem to be saying that . . .'
- Confirming   'So, we agree that . . .'
- Testing   'Would it be right to say that . . . ?'
- Summarizing   'So, your group appears to have identified the main issues as . . .'

Activity: Review your listening skills

The purpose of this activity is to review your listening skills. Choose a recent example of a conversation between you and a team member. Review this process using the following questions:

- What went well?
- What could be improved?
- What did I learn about my listening skills?
- What will I do differently next time?

You may find it helpful to review this process with the team member, as this will enable you to gain another perspective on your feedback skills. You may find it helpful to discuss your findings with your manager or mentor, and to identify ways in which you could improve your listening skills.

Presentation skills

Team leaders are regularly called upon to make presentations and these may range from informal presentations to colleagues to formal presentations to senior managers. Developing effective presentation skills is very important as you may be called on to make a presentation in a variety of situations such as:

- introducing a new idea or project to your team
- promoting ideas or products to customers or colleagues
- promoting your team and its work to other colleagues in the ILS
- during a training event or conference.

Successful presentations are important because they will enable you to communicate clearly with your team members, colleagues and customers. Presentation skills are also important for communicating with the wider profession, e.g. at conferences, and also they are often part of interview procedures. There are a number of areas to consider when embarking on a presentation: planning and preparation; the use of visual aids; rehearsal and delivery; working with a co-presenter; and dealing with questions.

Planning the presentation

Though invisible to an audience, planning and preparation are essential components of any good presentation. You need to begin by thinking about the overall purpose and the specific objectives of your presentation. What is the main message that you want someone to take away from your presentation? Once this is clear then it will help you to structure and organize your presentation.

Initial questions to consider include:

- Who are your audience, what are their expectations from the presentation and what is their current knowledge of the topic?
- Where is the venue and what equipment will be available?
- What time is available for the presentation? How can you make the best use of it?
- What is your main message?
- What other information do you need to convey to meet your objectives?
- What approach(es) could you use to present the topic and material in a clear, interesting and involving way?
- How formal or informal should your delivery of the material be?
- Is it appropriate to involve your audience in activities?
- What handouts, visual, audio or audiovisual aids could reinforce the content? When should they be used?
- How will you gain audience feedback? By inviting questions? When?

Preparing the presentation

Preparing the presentation involves identifying the structure and the main points that you need to get over to your audience. A standard structure for a presentation includes an introduction, a middle section or main body, and a conclusion.

Introduction

This normally takes up no more than 10% of the available time and in the introduction you need to:

- introduce yourself
- clearly outline the main purpose of your presentation, the subject of the presentation and its overall structure
- motivate the audience to listen by pointing out what they will gain from the presentation.
- include any housekeeping announcements, e.g. health and safety notices
- capture the attention of the audience (for example, through a story, a quotation, a question).

Main section

This typically forms about 80% of the presentation and in it you should:

- outline your subject and present it in three to five main chunks
- lead the audience from the known to the unknown
- make sure that your information is up to date and correct
- use examples and anecdotes
- use images, graphs and photographs.

Common errors that are made in presentations include: providing too much detail, attempting to cover too many topics and using examples that are not of interest or relevant to the audience.

The conclusion

This should take about 10% of the time and should:

- summarize the key ideas
- end on a positive note
- thank the audience
- provide them with appropriate contact information, e.g. your e-mail address.

If you have decided to involve the audience actively then you will need to decide what form the involvement will take and how it will fit into the presentation's structure. Example activities include asking the audience to discuss a topic with their neighbour; asking them to complete some kind of questionnaire; inviting questions from the audience. You will need to think about how much time to spend on the activity and what you will do if the activity does not work.

Visual aids

Good visual aids support or reinforce the presentation and they should add interest, variety and impact to a presentation. Any visual aids you use should:

- be relevant
- complement and enhance the presentation
- help the audience understand the topic
- be professional in appearance and presentation.

Nowadays it is standard practice to use presentation software such as PowerPoint and if you don't already know how to use this software then it is worthwhile investing a little time in getting to grips with the basic facilities. Guidelines for layout of PowerPoint slides include:

- Limit the text to no more than seven rows per slide and seven words per row.
- Use standard styles and fonts for text, not smaller than 18 point in size.
- Use a clear, light background with dark text. Make sure that there is a sharp contrast between text and background.

Case study 6.3   Presentation on customer-service skills

One of the advantages of using software such as PowerPoint is that you can include images, audio and videotape clips.

A team leader was asked to make a presentation on customer-service skills to another team within her ILS. Using digital audio recording equipment she interviewed a few customers and then presented their comments as part of her presentation. This process took a couple of hours to organize but helped increase the impact of the overall presentation.

When you are using PowerPoint remember to take a paper copy of your slides with you. It is useful to print out slides six to a page as this helps you to know where you are in the presentation and also what is to come next.

Other available aids include:

- handouts
- flipcharts or whiteboards

- smart boards
- physical objects and product displays
- photographic slides
- simple sound systems
- video playback.

Whatever aids you choose, you need to check before the presentation that the venue is suitable for their use and that the necessary equipment is available and working. Even then, it is prudent to have contingency plans ready in case of equipment failure! If you are using PowerPoint it is worthwhile having copies on a disk, USB and CD. You may also want to have a set of acetates as backup. If you are using audio or video clips and making a presentation on unfamiliar equipment it is worthwhile bringing along two copies of your presentation: a copy that contains all images, audio clips and videos; and a stripped down version that will work even if the ICT facility is fairly basic. Run through the presentation on the equipment that you will be using on the day. Expect equipment to fail and have a contingency plan.

Rehearsal and delivery

If you are not experienced as a presenter it is a good idea to rehearse your presentation, e.g. to trusted colleagues or at home to family, friends or even the dog or cat. Rehearsal is essential to check the timing of your presentation, to enable you to become familiar with presenting your information orally, to enable you to develop fluent use of the presentation aids, and to reinforce your confidence in both materials and delivery. Practice really does make perfect – and the more you rehearse, the better the end result is likely to be. Practise delivering the presentation aloud rather than silently. Use a tape recorder or a video to record yourself and then think about how you could improve the presentation. Effective presentations are those that have been well prepared and are delivered with confidence and enthusiasm.

Key points for effective delivery include:

- Dress appropriately – smartness instils confidence in both audience and speaker. If in doubt about the dress code then dress formally in a suit or with a smart jacket rather than more informal clothes.
- Arrive in time to make any checks and to organize your materials and equipment without haste or confusion.
- Have a printout of your presentation.
- Aim for a natural, confident and relaxed posture and delivery.
- Avoid distracting mannerisms.
- Use eye contact to draw all parts of the audience into the presentation.
- Show interest and enthusiasm in your tone and manner throughout.
- Speak more slowly and carefully than you would in normal conversation.

Pace is important. You are familiar with your material; the audience is not.

- Project and pitch your voice so that everyone can hear you easily, and vary your expression appropriately.
- Stand clear of visuals when referring to them to ensure that everyone can see them.
- Face the audience when talking about a visual aid – don't turn your back on them and talk to the screen.
- If you make mistakes then correct those relating to accuracy of content.
- Ignore those that are unlikely to be noticed and simply carry on.

Points to avoid:

- a word-for-word script – if you take one, you will read from it!
- a monotonous delivery tone
- humour (unless you are certain it is appropriate and will be well received).

Working with a co-presenter

If you are working with a co-presenter then you will need additional preparation and, as a team, you will need to work out:

- who will present which part of the content and its relation to the presentation overall
- when you will each speak and how you will pass over to each other
- where you will both stand or sit.

Each presenter needs to make a conscious effort to give unity and continuity to their presentation. For example, you need to devise appropriate 'handovers' from one person to the next, and to decide how and when questions will be dealt with. If you are presenting with another person then it is important to be in agreement with what you are going to say and how you are going to say it. Don't interrupt or disagree with each other during the presentation. Keep any disagreements off stage!

Case study 6.3   Working with a co-presenter

Jane and John were asked to make a presentation at a conference on their experiences of lecturing to large groups of students in their university. They spent some time planning the presentation and how they were going to deliver it. They produced the presentation plan shown in Table 6.4. Their plan shows that the same person starts and concludes the presentation. They take turns in presenting different aspects of the subject, but in the advantages and disadvantages section they work together. In this section, their PowerPoint presentation had advantages on the left and disadvantages on the right-hand side. The two presenters stood on the left (John) or right (Jane) of the room to repeat and emphasize this pattern. This helps to give a very professional and 'slick' look to their performance.

Table 6.4 Working with a co-presenter – presentation plan

Timing	Topic	Presenter
5 min.	Introduction to presenters. Introduction to topic. Reasons why we have been asked to deliver presentation.	Jane
5 min.	Background to our work as information skills trainers. Outline of our work in lecturing to large groups.	John
10 min.	Advantages and disadvantages of lecturing to large groups.	John (advantages) Jane (disadvantages)
10 min.	Use of technology	Jane
10 min.	Use of activities	John
5 min.	Any questions	John (lead) Jane
5 min.	Summary and closure	Jane

Dealing with questions

Handling difficult questions is made easier by realizing that you are in control. It is up to you to decide when you will accept questions, e.g. during or at the end of a presentation. Inexperienced presenters often find it easier to take questions at the end of the presentation so as not to break their flow. The following general tips will help you answer any type of question:

- Listen carefully to the question. You need to listen to the actual words and also the emotions behind the question. Often the body language of the questioner will give you some useful information.
- If you are not sure about the meaning of the question then ask for clarification.
- Repeat the question in your own words. This will allow the whole audience to hear the question and it also allows you to check that you have fully understood the question.
- Answer the question to the best of your ability.
- If you don't know the answer then be honest and say that you don't know the answer. You may then want to ask if anyone in the audience can answer it or you may offer to e-mail the answer.
- Signal how many questions that you will take, e.g. at the end of your presentation say that there is time for three or four questions.
- When you want to close the session say that there is time for one more question and then after that question you must move on.

Sometimes tricky situations arise in question time and Table 6.5 provides examples of such situations and makes suggestions as to how they can be tackled. Finally, signal the end of question time by saying there is time for one more question and once that has been answered then move on to the closure of your presentation.

Table 6.5   Handling tricky situations during question time

Tricky situation	Strategy for dealing with it
You ask if there are any questions and you are met with a wall of silence.	Count up to ten in your head. This will help give people a chance to think through and articulate their question. • Accept that there are no questions and invite people to contact you later if they have any questions arising later. Move on to the closure of your presentation. • Ask people to talk with their neighbour and to identify any questions they have. Give them a few minutes for discussion and then ask for questions again.
Someone asks a question that has nothing to do with your presentation.	Thank them for the question. Say that it is beyond the scope of your presentation and advise them how they can get their question answered. For example, 'That is an interesting question but we are not covering that topic today. Perhaps we could talk about it after the session or in the coffee break.'
Someone asks a bizarre question.	Thank them for the question. Say that it is an interesting/unusual viewpoint. If you can't comment on it then say so.
Someone asks a question that is insulting, e.g. it is sexist, racist or offensive to a particular group of people.	Say that the question is likely to offend people and that this unacceptable. You may want to add that you personally feel extremely uncomfortable with the language used in the question. Move on to the next question.
Someone asks a challenging question, e.g. criticizes your library, project, service.	Thank them for raising the issue. Suggest that this isn't the right forum for raising the issue. Suggest that they talk to you in private after the event and you will help them to progress their issue, e.g. through the complaints procedure.
Two or more people in the audience disagree with each other. A public argument starts to take place.	Interrupt their discussion. Say that there are clearly different points of view in the audience. Say that there is insufficient time to explore the issue in more depth. Move on to the next question or start to end your presentation. For example, 'It's clear that there are a number of different points of view here. We can't discuss them in any more detail but perhaps individuals would like to follow them up after the session or in the coffee break.'

Using virtual communication tools

Nowadays virtual communication tools are widely used in the workplace and the purpose of this section is to review good practice in the use of common tools such as e-mail, discussion groups and chat conference rooms.

E-mail

E-mails are a common and simple method of exchanging information. Informal e-mail communication between staff where information and ideas are exchanged is possibly one of the most popular means of keeping up to date and solving small queries that arise everyday in the workplace. Many team leaders rely on e-mail as a way of informally communicating with their team members and colleagues on a variety of day-to-day matters. Before sending an e-mail it is worthwhile thinking about whether or not it is the most appropriate way of communicating with the other person. In general, personal and sensitive issues are best discussed face-to-face or over the phone.

As team leader it is important to encourage and support good practice in the use of e-mail in the workplace. This involves ensuring that everyone:

- uses a clear subject title for each e-mail
- writes their e-mail in a professional manner
- responds to messages quickly, e.g. an acknowledgement within 48 hours
- organizes their e-mails into appropriately named folders
- keeps their mailbox up to date
- uses the personal address book
- uses distribution lists
- uses the out-of-office facility.

E-mails are so commonplace at work that little attention is paid to how they are used. It is perhaps worthwhile reflecting on the tone used in e-mails. Some people and organizations have an extremely informal style with respect to e-mails, and if this is the case in your organization it is worthwhile thinking about whether or not this style is appropriate for external customers. Many people expect a minimum standard and this is likely to include: a salutation (Dear XXX or Hello XXX), some form of pleasantry, a closure (Yours sincerely or Many thanks) followed by signature. The style used in e-mails also varies from country to country. If you are in doubt as to the appropriate style it is probably best to be formal rather than too informal.

Online discussion groups or bulletin boards

Online discussion groups are now extensively used within many organizations and also information and library professional associations often host and support a large number of groups. Discussion groups enable individuals to communicate with each other under various topic headings. This is an asynchronous communication method, i.e. different individuals will come online at different times and respond to messages that were posted earlier that day or week. When you are online in a discussion group you can read and respond to other people's messages. If you need time to think or compose a long message then you can leave the virtual environment, think about your response and then go back online and reply. It is possible to cut and paste text, e.g. from Word documents into discussion group messages. This is useful as it means you can prepare your messages offline and then cut and paste them into the discussion group site. It is important to remember that any messages sent to a discussion group are permanently visible to everyone who has access to the group. If you want to send private messages then use e-mail.

Netiquette is the term used to describe the etiquette involved in virtual communications and here are some general guidelines in good practice:

- Thank, acknowledge and support people freely.
- Acknowledge before differing.
- Speak from own perspective.
- Avoid flaming spirals.
- CAPITAL letters are equivalent to shouting – don't use them.
- Red font colour is also equivalent to shouting – don't use it.
- Keep messages short. Longer messages need to be presented as an attachment so people can choose to read them at leisure.
- Don't respond to a message if you are experiencing strong negative feelings. Give yourself time to cool down. Then respond.

Chat or conference rooms

Chat or conference software enables the user and the ILS staff to hold a 'live' discussion by sending each other short written messages. The live discussion could be between a team leader and colleagues, or between library staff and customers, or it could be between two members of staff in different libraries. Chat software may be used to support individual users, provide quick advice and guidance to a member of staff, e.g. someone at a remote library, or as a coaching tool. Chat software normally enables public and/or private conversations to take place and, depending on the software, these may be with individuals or groups. Chats may take place in public chat arenas or else in private. Some chat software enables individual chat rooms to be set up so that different people can meet in different virtual places. Virtual learning environments include chat or conference software that enables these synchronous conversations to take place, and tools such as whiteboards may support them.

Chatting online has a number of advantages because it can be a private form of communication, it is immediate and the text can be saved for future reference. Chatting online can be helpful for people with hearing or speaking impairments and it can also ease communication among those for whom English is a second language. In addition the text of chat sessions can be used for training purposes. As with most tools there are disadvantages to online chat: these include the absence of non-verbal signals and the need to learn how to send and be comfortable with short telegraphic messages between two or more people. Some people don't feel comfortable with this form of communication and there is the potential danger that the other person may log-off and 'disappear'. However, an increasing number of people are becoming very experienced with this form of communication and there is an entire internet subculture built around chat.

The following tips may be used for communicating in chat or conference rooms:

- Appoint a chair person if there are more than four people in the conference.
- Signal when you want to speak using a question mark (?). The chairperson then invites you to speak.
- Send short messages.
- If you want to send a long message then split it into chunks and indicate that a message continues using a series of full stops (. . .).
- Limit your conference room sessions, e.g. no more than an hour or one item of business. Most people find chat sessions demand high levels of concentration.

Tips for joining a conference include:

- When you enter a conference room and other people are already present then you will not be able to see the discussions that took place before you arrived.
- Indicate your presence with a 'Hello'.
- Wait a minute or two so that you can understand some of the context of the conversation.
- Once you feel ready then plunge in and get going.

Summary

This chapter provides an outline of the communication skills required by team leaders and supervisors. The main message within this chapter is that it is important to choose the most appropriate communication tool for a particular situation. In addition, whatever the method of communication it is important to spend time planning and preparing how you are going to communicate with the individual or whole team. In particular, care must be taken in dealing with difficult or challenging situations, when it is normally best to talk with the person or whole team face to face.

Reference

Charvet, S. R. (1997) *Words that Change Minds: mastering the language of influence*, Dubugue IO, Kendall/Hunt Publishing Company.
Leigh, A. and Walters, M. (1998) *Effective change*, 2nd edn, London, CIPD.

7 Managing and leading complex teams

Introduction

Team leaders and supervisors may be asked to lead a complex team or, as a result of their role, they may be asked to join such a team or project. The purpose of this chapter is to consider some of the challenges involved in managing and leading different types of complex teams. This includes partnership teams which may be multi-professional, i.e. made up of representatives from different professional groups, or teams involving members from different organizations (who may be from the same or different professional backgrounds); diverse teams where members may come from a wide range of national and cultural backgrounds; and also virtual teams. This chapter will help you to lead or to be an active and effective team member in a complex team.

Working in collaborative and multi-professional teams

> Partnership is one of the most complex and difficult ways in which to work. When it works even reasonably well, however, it can bring some of the best results for the end-user.
>
> Dakers (2003, 47)

Information and library workers have always had a tradition of networking and collaborative working both within the profession and also with other professional groups. In the last decade, governments, agencies and organizations have raised the profile of partnership working as they see this as one way of meeting the needs to modernize and develop new approaches to working and delivering services in a complex and rapidly changing environment. A scan of the current ILS literature reveals that many information workers are now involved in developing and delivering a wide range of services through partnerships. Pilling and Kenna (2002) provide an overview of many collaborative projects and partnerships in the information and library world.

Sullivan and Skelcher (2002) highlight the rise in collaborative working between public, private and the voluntary and community sectors and they map out how collaboration is central to the way in which public policy is made, managed and delivered in the UK. Partnership working is currently popular with the UK government where it is seen as an important strategy for tackling complex and interlinked issues such as crime, education, health and housing in our inner cities.

Partnership working is one way in which the modernization agenda is being tackled and it involves collaboration with partnerships in health and social care, social inclusion, and education which includes a lifelong learning agenda involving many public and other information and library services. Financial drivers are often used to ensure that the different sectors and agencies work together in partnership to deliver services and products.

What are the benefits of working in partnership? Informal discussions with some directors of information and library services and also with project managers produced the following list of benefits of this type of work:

- Enhanced access to people, resources and organizations.
- Enhanced ownership. Projects that are set up to tackle specific problems collaboratively are owned by the partners and this means that the project outcomes are more likely to be accepted and owned by the partner organizations.
- Enhanced quality. The involvement of a wide range of people who bring their different professional perspectives can enhance the quality of the project experience and outcomes. Individual partners may be more willing to take on new ideas and working practices as a result of the partnership.
- Increased exposure to new ideas/approaches. Working in multi-professional teams can help partners to broaden their outlook and obtain a broader understanding of their work and their context.
- Improved use of resources. Partnership working can enhance access to resources and also enable more efficient use of resources.
- Enhanced motivation. Being part of a successful partnership can boost morale and help individuals to develop new enthusiasm for their work. However, the opposite may be true too!
- Continuous professional development. Working on a collaborative project provides individual workers with the opportunity to develop their knowledge and skills.

Partnership working does bring learning opportunities for the different partners and this can be the result of 'enforced' reflection on our own perspectives and working practices in comparison with those of our partners. Despite these benefits there are some challenges to working in and leading partnership teams. These challenges to successful teamwork may be the result of:

- long-held rivalries or competition
- different values and beliefs
- power struggles
- differing perceptions and perspectives
- potential commitment of large amounts of time, resources and energy
- differences in systems and procedures

- differences in organizational cultures
- responses of people or organizations *not* involved in the partnership.

Case study 7.1   SureStart

In the UK the development of a wide range of government initiatives, e.g. Education Action Zones, SureStart and Connexions, has resulted in some information workers being involved in innovative team and project work in collaboration with other professional workers. These initiatives sometimes lead to the development of a new form of work organization where a project is made up of a series of teams and each team is a multi-professional team. In this situation a team leader with responsibility for a team is likely to be working with individuals who may or may not be employed by the project and may be line-managed by other staff, e.g. public library managers, even though they are physically located and work within the project. This type of teamwork can be extremely rewarding and also very stressful.

Discussions with a number of information and library workers involved in a SureStart project in a northern city in the UK identified a number of challenges. SureStart is a UK government programme which aims to achieve better outcomes for children, parents and communities. This SureStart project was made up of staff from different agencies such as health, social services, lifelong learning (including public libraries) as well as voluntary sector organizations. The line managers of these staff were not the SureStart project manager or team leaders who were often involved in lengthy negotiations with different agencies concerning working practices. Even the simplest situation, e.g. what happened on the morning of the state occasion of the Queen Mother's funeral, was made complex because the project manager and team leaders had to manage the situation where different people were on different types of contractual arrangements. In reality this meant that their working practices varied so that some staff were given the morning off work, others an hour off work, while others had no time off for this national event. The team leaders had little say in what could happen on that morning as the staff they 'managed' were all line-managed by different managers working in different agencies each with its own custom and practices.

Another example that demonstrates the complexity of working on this type of project is the matter of identity. 'Who are we and who is our employer?' is a deceptively simple question. However, individual team members, team leaders and also the project manager had different employers. Some people were employed by the local authority and then seconded to the project for 12 months. Other workers were employed by the project while some people had their salaries paid by other agencies but were entirely based within the project. Issues such as name badges raised fierce discussion as some workers wanted to wear their employer's badges, others the project badge and some wore both badges. The project manager and team leaders explored issues of identity, their own and that of the project, and then used these discussions as the basis for discussions within their teams and the project as a whole. Over a year the issue of identity became less important as the teams and whole project developed their own identity.

In this type of partnership work it is essential that team leaders and project managers have the necessary support. In this example, the project team leader made extensive use of mentoring support and also a management development programme as a means of providing herself with time and space to reflect on the challenges of managing a collaborative multi-professional team. In addition, she involved all of the team leaders in this development process and this enabled them to work together and tackle many challenging issues.

Sullivan and Skelcher (2002) identify and explore different ways of conceptualizing the processes of working in partnership and they have identified its life cycle, presented in Figure 7.1. This life cycle for partnership teams is based on the development of collaboration as a series of consecutive stages:

- Preconception. The potential partners, agencies and individuals become aware of the possibility of working in partnership and the potential benefits and needs to do so.
- Initiation. Individuals come together and explore the potential of working together in partnership.
- Formalization. The partnership is formalized by implementing an appropriate governance structure and/or committing to the partnership.
- Operation. The partnership is put into action and partners work together to achieve the partnership goals.
- Termination. The partnership closes or transforms itself into another venture.

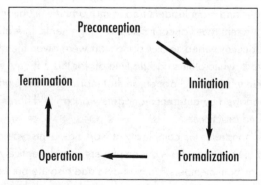

Figure 7.1
Life cycle of partnership working

This model provides a useful template for exploring and facilitating partnership arrangements; its structure is similar to that of the stages of team development (see Chapter 2). As with the team development model, it is perhaps an oversimplification. Some potential partnerships will not move beyond the preconception stage and may stall at the initiation stage. Others may transform into a new venture during the formalization stage when individuals develop a better understanding of their context and the project potential. Overall, this model does help to provide team leaders with guidance on how to facilitate working in partnership and this concept is explored later in this chapter.

Leading and managing the partnership team

The literature on partnership and collaborative working provides a set of characteristics that distinguish effective partnerships from those that are not effective and, perhaps, fail. Effective partnerships tend to demonstrate the following characteristics:

- The project goal and objectives are clear.
- The goal and objectives are shared by all partners.
- All partners have made a commitment to the project.
- There is trust and respect among different partners.
- The partnership process is transparent and agreed by all the partners.
- The action plan is realistic and takes into account the needs of the partners.
- Partners share the workload and give each other support.
- There is clear and open communication between partners.
- Partners give and take constructive feedback.
- There is a clear framework of responsibility and accountability.
- Partners invest time into the partnership and their relationships with each other.

The following list identifies some of the characteristics of partnerships that fail:

- **Domination of the partnership by one member or organization**. If one dominant partner takes over then this can lead to resentment by other members. It may lead to individual members not feeling part of the team and withdrawing from the project.
- **Cynical members**. Some partners may be cynical about the project, its funding or working in partnership. This may have a negative effect on the partnership and result in a self-fulfilling prophecy.
- **Rotating members**. This is a problem if one or more partners are represented at meetings by different members of staff throughout the life of the project. This means that the team rarely gets beyond the forming stage and there has to be a constant repetition of previous discussions in order to enable the new members to catch up.
- **Previous history**. Sometimes the past history of the relationships between partner organizations or individuals can have a detrimental effect on the whole partnership. This is particularly true if members use the current project to sort out old scores and battles.
- **Unequal distribution or work or responsibilities**. If a small number of people take on the majority of the work then this can lead to them feeling resentful as they are 'carrying' other team members. It can also mean that other team members begin to lose ownership of the project.
- **Added bureaucracy**. Working in partnership can add another level of bureaucracy. Partnership working tends to involve more meetings and careful documentation of events. This can often take up more time and resources than necessary.

- **Different cultures**. A potential problem area is the different cultures and working patterns of project partners. This issue is discussed in Chapter 8. Unless these are respected then unnecessary conflict may develop in the project.
- **Inexperienced partnership manager**. The appointment of a partnership or project manager with little experience of working on projects, working across sectors or working in an intensely political context can sometimes lead to the demise of a project.
- **Political interference**. Political interference, e.g. by senior managers, directors and elected members, can lead to problems for the partnership.

The initial stages of a partnership are probably the most crucial ones in terms of creating a strong foundation for effective working. The more partners and more complex the project the greater amount of time and attention to detail needs to be paid to the initial stages. Dakers (2003, 47) identifies the 'lead time' (the length of time taken to set up and run projects) and she states 'organizations considering this complex level of collaboration should allow significantly more lead time than for projects with fewer partners. No doubt we will produce the results to time, but we will all be somewhat greyer for it'.

As with any team (see Chapters 2, 5 and 6) the first few meetings of partners may involve the following processes:

- introductions
- surfacing expectations, hopes and fears
- creating the vision
- building the objectives
- agreeing the action plan.

The process of surfacing expectations is a simple and yet very important one. Asking partners what they expect as part of being on the team will enable similar and also different expectations to be aired and discussed. It will also help to prevent small issues growing and causing tensions within the partnership.

Case study 7.2   Collaborative lifelong learning project
I was involved in a collaborative lifelong learning project which involved staff from six different organizations and a number of different professional groups, i.e. information and library workers, community development workers, teachers, IT technicians and administrators. During the 'surfacing of expectations' activity it became clear that different people had very different expectations as to the length and timing of meetings that they would be involved in. In part these differences related to the working practices of their parent organizations. For some team members it was very important to end meetings by 5 p.m. at the very latest while other people anticipated (and were quite

happy about the idea) that meetings would run through until 6 or 7 p.m. After some discussion the group agreed that all meetings would end by 5 p.m. at the very latest. The discussion and decision helped to prevent conflict at a later stage in the project process.

Once a partnership team is established then it is vitally important that all members are kept on board and engage with the project. This is one of the key roles of the team manager who must create and maintain the 'glue' that holds everything together. The complex team 'glue' may involve either informal or formal processes and these are divided into 'soft' (or people-centred) approaches and 'hard' (or procedural and documented) approaches. These are outlined in Table 7.1. Both types of project team 'glue' are important. Effective partnership team leaders and

Table 7.1 Types of complex team glue

Soft	Hard
• shared goal(s)	• minutes of meetings
• shared values and beliefs	• contracts
• common concerns and deeper convictions	• terms of reference
• meetings and social networking	• project schedules
• informal communications, e.g. e-mail or phone calls	• use of project management tools, e.g. Gantt charts
• informal feedback	• reporting regimes, e.g. reporting back to senior managers
• goodwill	• funding regimes
• people – such as project managers and project team members	• legal requirements

managers ensure that the partnership glue is in place and they will spend time nurturing both 'soft' and 'hard' glue. If the project comes across barriers or problems then the formal arrangements such as contracts and regular meetings may become vital to sorting out the situation and moving the project forward.

Case study 7.3   Of rocks and safe channels: learning to navigate as an inter-professional team

Bateman et al. (2003, 143) describe an inter-professional primary care team that was established to serve a new community in Cambridgeshire. The new team included doctors, nurses, a pharmacist, a well-family services co-ordinator, an information officer (a qualified and experienced librarian), a service development manager, a research and learning officer, a patient participant co-ordinator, an information technologist plus four administrative staff. The team development process involved the embryo team working on and identifying five essential principles for the team. These were:

- Professionals with relevant expertise and experience outside primary care were sought and encouraged to maintain strong links with their 'base' profession
- A 'flat' management style was adopted by the new team
- All team members were to be encouraged to become 'curious' and were to be given the encouragement and the tools with which to learn
- All team members were to be encouraged to use their particular skills and expertise to offer enhanced patient care
- All team members were to be encouraged to recognize the importance of establishing respectful and responsible relationships with patients so that patients could play a genuine part in the evolution of the health care services and the health care team.

Bateman et al. (2003, 144–8) identify and explore some of the issues that arose in the first year of work for this new team. These included:

- uncertainty over individual's own professional contribution and value
- difficulties in identifying training requirements for individuals due to the unique nature of their roles
- the need for guidance and mentoring to team members from specialists from their own professional background
- professional partner expectations.

The solutions to these issues arose through a combination of discussions within the team and also with colleagues and organizations outside the team. It involved an iterative process of day-to-day engagement with the issue and also conscious reflection on it. The authors write:

The analogy of navigation through rocks and safe channels was felt to be highly appropriate by team members as they reflected back on this paper and on the first year. Observations were made by team members about the lack of a defined course which one could follow ('uncharted waters' for each individual and for the team as a whole), about the unexpected and initially ill-defined nature of many of the difficulties which arose ('hidden rocks' of unknown scale and range), and about the importance of a shared vision within the team (pulling constructively together through rougher waters).

Bateman et al. (2003, 147)

Activity: Review your experience of working in a partnership team

This activity is aimed at team leaders and supervisors who have experience of either leading or membership of a partnership team. The purpose of this activity is to review your experience of working in a particular partnership team. Reflect on this experience and review the process using the following questions:

- What went well?
- What could be improved?
- What did I learn about my ability to lead or participate in a partnership team?
- What should I do differently next time I am working in a partnership team?

You may find it helpful to review this process with other members from the partnership team, as this will enable you to gain another perspective. You may find it helpful to discuss your findings with your manager or mentor, and to identify ways in which you could improve your ability to engage with working in partnership.

Leading and managing diverse teams

> The office of today (and even more so of tomorrow) consists of people of many different cultures working together. Appreciating and being able to manage cultural differences at home and abroad is becoming more and more part of everyone's job.
>
> Schneider and Barsoux (1997, vii)

Teamwork frequently involves working together with people from different cultures, different countries and perhaps generations. The concept of working in diverse teams has developed in recent years. Kandola and Fullerton introduce the idea of managing diversity as follows:

> The basic concept of managing diversity accepts the workforce consists of a diverse population of people. The diversity consists of visible and non-visible differences which will include factors such as sex, age, background, race, disability and work style. It is founded on the premise that harnessing these differences will create a productive environment in which everyone feels valued, where their talents are being fully utilized and their organisational goals are met.
>
> Kandola and Fullerton (1994, 8)

Schneider and Barsoux (1997) suggest that working in diverse teams involves recognizing and understanding the underlying cultural assumptions that give rise to different values and beliefs about work, working with others and management. Culture is extremely deep-rooted and includes unconscious values, e.g. about ways of behaving with other people, and different practices, e.g. rituals, heroes and symbols, and ways of being. There is an extensive research base on culture and management, and this was reviewed by Korac-Kakabadse et al. (2001). A commonly used approach to working in diverse teams comes from the work of Hofstede (1994) who identifies six layers of culture which he presents as country level (where we live or have lived); regional and/or ethnic and/or religious and/or linguistic affiliation level; gender level; generation level, e.g. teenagers, young professionals, over 70s; social class level associated with educational opportunities, occupation or profession; and finally organizational or corporate level (for those who are employed).

Hofstede identifies five cultural dimensions that managers need to take into account when they are working in diverse teams:

- **Individualism**. The extent to which people think of themselves as individuals or members of a group. In individualistic countries such as France, Germany or Canada people are expected to look after themselves and important values to them are personal time, freedom and challenge. This is in contrast to collectivist cultures such as Japan, Korea or Greece where individuals are bonded through strong relationship ties based on loyalty, e.g. to the family, team or employer, and the team or group is considered more important than the individual.
- **Power distance**. This is concerned with the distance between managers and workers and the importance of hierarchy. In high power-distance countries such as Latin America and many Asian and African countries, workers tend to be afraid of their managers and leaders (who tend to be paternalistic and autocratic) and treat them with respect. In contrast, in low power-distance countries (such as the USA, the UK and most of Europe) workers are more likely to challenge their managers who will tend to use a consultative management style.
- **Gender**. In countries such as the USA, Japan, Hong Kong and the UK (where the masculine index is high), people tend to value challenging work, opportunities for gaining a high income, personal recognition for their work, and opportunities for advancement to a higher-level job. In countries such as Sweden, France, Israel and Denmark (where feminine values are more important) people tend to value good working relationships, co-operative behaviours and long-term job security.
- **Certainty dimension**. This relates to the extent to which people prefer unstructured and unpredictable environments as opposed to structured and predictable ones. Cultures with a strong uncertainty dimension such as South Korea and Japan will tend to avoid unknown situations, which they will perceive as threatening. In contrast, in countries such as the UK, USA, Netherlands, Singapore and Hong Kong where uncertainty avoidance is weak then people feel less threatened by unknown situations. They are also more likely to be open to innovations, risk, etc.

- **Time orientation**. Countries such as China, Hong Kong, Japan and Taiwan demonstrate a long-term time orientation that is characterized by persistence, perseverance, a respect for a hierarchy of the status of relationships, thrift and a sense of shame. In contrast, countries such as the UK, Canada, Germany and Australia have a short-term orientation marked by a sense of security and stability, a protection of one's reputation, a respect for tradition and a reciprocation of favours.

The implication of this model for any team leader is to be aware that if your team is made up of people from different cultures then they are likely to have different approaches to their work. Individuals who are experienced in working within a collectivist culture are likely to find that they are on familiar territory with collaborative team work but they may feel exposed if asked to work in an extremely individualist manner. In contrast, a team that is predominately made up of information workers from countries with a low power-distance may inadvertently exclude a team worker from a high power-distance country who is not familiar with or comfortable with the rest of their team's relationship with their manager which includes challenge. At the same time, a team leader may enjoy working with uncertainty and ambiguity during a change process and may find it frustrating that other workers, e.g. from cultures with a strong uncertainty dimension, want high levels of structure imposed on their work.

Hofstede's work is useful because it reminds us that different people have different needs and will work and relate to each other in very different ways. The danger with this type of categorization is that it will be used to stereotype and label people. There are vast differences between people coming from the same type of cultural background as much as there are between people from different cultural backgrounds. The mobility of people means that a team may be made up of individuals who were born in one country, educated in schools in another country, received a university education in another country and are now living and working in a different country. Attempting to label such a person with a 'neat' label of the type used by Hofstede is oversimplistic and unhelpful. The key message for team leaders is to get to know your team and the individuals within it. You will then be able to adapt your management style to take into account the different needs of individual team workers.

Case study 7.4   How do you answer the phone?

I was asked to facilitate a training day on customer care skills for the information and library services team of an international organization. The team was made up of staff representing more than 12 countries. One of the activities during the day focused on exploring ways of providing a consistent and high-quality information service. During this activity I asked the question 'How do you answer the phone?' This led to a lengthy discussion where it soon became evident that the way in which team members answered the phone varied hugely depending on their nationality. Telephone responses ranged from 'Hello' to someone providing their name, job title, name of their section and name of the ILS. Everyone felt quite strongly that their approach to answering the phone was the correct one. After some discussion during the workshop and then follow-up work by the team leader, the team developed a customer care policy plus guidelines on working practices. One of these guidelines included detailed guidance on how to answer the phone. The guide included three preferred ways of answering the phone and this approach acknowledged the differences between staff from different cultures and at the same time laid down a set of minimum standards.

Case study 7.5   Different time visions

My own academic research is in the area of virtual teamwork (see Allan, 2006). I am particularly interested in the concept of time visions, i.e. the idea that people from different cultures have different approaches to time. Clock or calendar time is the dominant time vision in American, Anglo-Saxon, Germanic and Scandinavian countries. This approach is characterized by the use of diaries and calendars; time is often viewed as a commodity, illustrated by sentences such as 'I'll save time by . . .', and, in contrast to some other cultures, has a relatively short-term perspective. In contrast, very different approaches to time are found in eastern cultures, and these are called 'event', 'timeless' and 'harmonic' time visions. These approaches are continuous, multidimensional or recurrent, and long term. Differences in approaches to time appear in international team work when individuals have different approaches to meetings, e.g. arriving on time or when they are ready, separating out or merging work and private lives, 'going with the flow' or 'going with the clock'. Unless the team leader and members are aware of these differences then they can be the cause of tensions within a group. As a result, it is useful to talk about time and individual approaches to time and expectations at the start of the teamwork.

Activity: Review your experience of working in a diverse team

This activity is aimed at team leaders and supervisors who have experience of either leading or membership of a diverse team. The purpose of this activity is to review your experience of working in a particular diverse team. Reflect on this experience and review the process using the following questions:

* Were individual differences respected within the team?
* What could be improved?
* What did I learn about my ability to work in a diverse team?
* What should I do differently next time I am working in a diverse team?

You may find it helpful to review this process with other members from the diverse team, as this will enable you to gain another perspective. You may find it helpful to discuss your findings with your manager or mentor, and to identify ways in which you can improve your ability to work in diverse teams.

Virtual teams

Many team leaders are now involved in working in either an entirely virtual or a blended (a mixture of virtual and face-to-face) environment. In many respects working in a virtual environment is similar to working with partnership or diverse teams as the team development process may be quite lengthy. Sometimes virtual teamwork takes place entirely via e-mail. Virtual environments such as virtual learning environments, organizational intranet sites or online collaborative project sites are increasingly used as the communication centre for virtual teams. Table 7.2 illustrates some of the different communication tools used by different types of virtual teams.

Table 7.2   Different communication tools used by virtual teams

Note: adapted from Gillam and Oppenheim (2006)

Characteristics of team	Use of ICT
Teams that work at the same time and in different places	Online chats, videoconferencing, e-mail, telephone
Teams that work at different times and in the same place	Bulletin boards, e-mail, groupware, voicemail
Teams that work at different times and in different places	Bulletin boards, e-mail, groupware, fax, voicemail

Gillam and Oppenheim (2006) review virtual teams and refer to Duarte's and Snyder's classification of virtual teams which is based on the nature of the task being undertaken:

- Networked teams – working towards a common goal or purpose, often with diffuse and fluid membership according to the expertise required.
- Parallel teams – for specific tasks or assignments with distinct membership.
- Project or product development teams – for non-routine tasks with specific or measurable results and a clearly delineated membership.
- Work or production teams – regular and ongoing work in one functional area with clearly defined membership.
- Service teams – support roles using differences between time zones to their advantage.
- Management teams – across space and time (but not typically organizational boundaries) tackling issues as they arise.
- Action teams – immediate responses, often to emergencies.

Gillam and Oppenheim (2006, 161)

Salmon (2000) identifies the stages that a virtual group or team is likely to experience and these are presented in Table 7.3 (page 133) along with ways in which a team leader may intervene to ensure effective team work. In the first stage, access and motivation, it is the team leader's role to ensure that everyone has access to the virtual environment. This stage is sometimes time consuming and may involve a series of phone calls before everyone is working online. At this stage, it is vital that you have technical back-up that you can call on if complex problems arise.

Case study 7.6   Technical back-up in e-mentoring project

I was recently involved in an e-mentoring project involving over 100 participants. The first few weeks of the project were involved in ensuring that everyone had access to the project internet site. Fortunately, we had very good technical back-up to resolve issues with individuals arising from their organization's firewalls and internet access. However, we were unable to resolve the difficulties for one person, who worked for a national bank, and she ending up taking part in the virtual teamwork via an internet café.

The second stage involves online socialization where individuals get to know each other, find their virtual voice, and begin working together in a virtual environment. At this stage, individuals are often asked to share a brief biography or some other ice-breaker activity (see Allan, 2002; Lewis and Allan, 2004). If you are involved in establishing a virtual team then it is worthwhile spending some time establishing ground rules with the team. These are likely to include some of the following:

- Check the discussion group at agreed intervals. This may be daily, every few days or even weekly depending on the unit.
- Inform the group of any absences, e.g. due to annual leave.
- Keep messages concise and relevant.
- Keep one topic per message. This enables threads to develop.
- Encourage quieter members and 'lurkers' to join in.
- Acknowledge someone else's contribution and offer support.
- Ask for clarification about something you don't understand.
- Enhance acknowledgement by showing you understand what they say when you acknowledge. This is particularly important if you then want to disagree.
- If disagreeing then state first that you recognize that other opinions exist, then provide your own opinion. Don't just disagree or, even worse, claim someone is wrong.
- Give a rationale for your opinion. Allow others to see where you are coming from.
- Before posting your message think about how other people will read and interpret it. If in doubt ask a colleague for their feedback on your proposed response.

The third stage involves information exchange where team members are beginning to work together by exchanging relevant workplace information. At this stage, the role of the team leader is to encourage people to work together and this sometimes

Table 7.3 Stages in the life of a virtual team
Note: adapted from Salmon (2000)

Stage	Team leader activities
1. Access and motivation	• Ensure team members know how to access the online environment. • Welcome individuals as they enter the virtual environment. • Sort out any technical issues.
2. Online socialization	• Lead a round of introductions with, perhaps, an online ice-breaker. • Welcome new team members or late arrivals. • Provide a structure for getting started, e.g. agreement of group rules, netiquette. • If individuals break the agreed group netiquette then tackle them (either privately or through the discussion group). • Encourage quieter members to join in.
3. Information exchange	• Provide structured activities. • Encourage participation. • Ask questions. • Encourage team members to post short messages with longer items sent as attachments. • Provide summaries of online discussions. • Allocate online roles to individual members, e.g. to provide a summary of a particular thread of discussion. • Close threads as and when appropriate. • Encourage the virtual team to develop its own life and history. Welcome shared language, metaphors, rituals and jokes.
4. Performance	• Encourage team members to lead discussions. • Support individual 'risk'. • Encourage reflection on different activities.
5. End of team	• Highlight team achievements. • Encourage (structured) reflection on learning processes. • Encourage evaluation of online team experience. • Thank team members for their contributions and work. • Formally close the team site.

takes place via structured activities or by allocating or sharing specific roles. Sometimes there is an explosion of messages. (I know of one virtual team that produced over 23,000 messages in three weeks!) If this is the case, then the team leader can support the team by providing brief summaries. This is called weaving and involves summarizing and synthesizing the content of multiple responses in a virtual team.

The fourth stage is the performance stage when the virtual team is working effectively together. At this stage there is often little for the team leader to do except ensure that the team is on track and provide space and time for reflection. There is the danger that in today's pressured working world we will be overwhelmed by carrying out lots of activities with very short deadlines and being overloaded with input from e-mails and other sources. This is likely to be at the expense of a more reflective approach (this is discussed in Chapter 10 in the section on work/life balance). This is a particular problem for online work and so it means that it is very important for the team leader to encourage reflective and developmental activities.

The final and fifth stage is the end of the virtual team work and involves the team leader in recognizing and validating the team's achievements; encouraging reflection on the team experiences and individual learning; encouraging evaluation of the virtual team experience; and thanking team members for their contributions and work. Sometimes a virtual party is held complete with images of refreshments! Finally, the team leader needs to ensure that the site is formally closed.

Many teams now work in a blended manner, i.e. a mixture of face-to-face and virtual teamwork. Current practice suggests that it is best to start off the teamwork with a face-to-face meeting and then work with a mixture of virtual and face-to-face meetings and close the team with a face-to-face meeting. If it is possible to meet face-to-face only once then the general advice is to do that at the team-formation stage (Pauleen and Yoong, 2001). The timeline for this type of blended practice is shown in Figure 7.2. An important component of effective teamwork is the development of trust within the team. Boden and Molotoch (1994) suggest that it is important to 'upgrade' from virtual to other means of communication, e.g. phone or face-to-face, if you are dealing with difficult situations; they call this the 'compulsion of proximity'. This suggests that team leaders need to spend time developing trust within the virtual and blended team, and they may need to take 'time out' to communicate with each other by other means. This is illustrated in Case study 7.7.

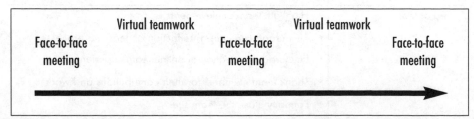

Figure 7.2 Timeline for blended teamwork

Case study 7.7   Challenges in a blended team
I once worked as a team member in a blended team working together to organize information skills training in a university. We had face-to-face meetings organized at monthly intervals. In between meetings, a disagreement blew up online and it was clear that there was a serious disagreement between a few team members. The team leader organized an additional face-to-face meeting and ensured that those people who were most embroiled in the debate were able to attend. The issues were resolved fairly easily once everyone sat around a table together.

Activity: Review your experience of working in a virtual team

This activity is aimed at team leaders and supervisors who have experience of either leading or membership of a virtual team. The purpose of this activity is to review your experience of working in a particular virtual team. Reflect on this experience and review the process using the following questions:

- What went well?
- What could be improved?
- What did I learn about my ability to lead or participate in a virtual team?
- What should I do differently next time I am working in a virtual team?

You may find it helpful to review this process with other members from the partnership team, as this will enable you to gain another perspective. You may find it helpful to discuss your findings with your manager or mentor, and to identify ways in which you can improve your ability to engage with working in a virtual team.

Summary

This chapter is concerned with complex teams. The benefits and challenges of working in complex teams such as diverse teams, collaborative teams, multi-professional teams and virtual teams are explored and illustrated with examples and case studies. Team leaders need to spend time creating and maintaining effective complex teams by developing the 'glue' that holds the project together. This involves active engagement into 'soft' or people-centred approaches and also ensuring that there are enabling 'hard' practices such as contracts, terms of reference and other documentation.

References

Allan, B. (2002) *E-learning and Teaching in Library and Information Services*, London, Facet Publishing.

Allan, B. (2006) Time to learn? E-learners' experiences of time in virtual learning communities, *Management Learning*, accepted for publication July 2006.

Bateman, H., Bailey, P. and McLellan, H. (2003) Of Rocks and Safe Channels: learning to navigate as an inter-professional team, *Journal of Interprofessional Care*, **17** (2), 2003.

Boden, D. and Molotoch, H. L. (1994) The Compulsion of Proximity. In Friedland, R. and Boden, D. (eds) *NowHere Space, Time and Modernity*, Berkeley CA, University of California Press, 257–86.

Dakers, H. (2003) The BL Reaches Out, *Library and Information Update*, **2** (10), 46–7.

Gillam, C. and Oppenheim, C. (2006) Reviewing the Impact of Virtual Teams in the Information Age, *Journal of Information Science*, **32** (2), 160–75.

Hofstede, G. (1994) *Cultures and Organizations*, London, HarperCollins.

Kandola, R. and Fullerton, J. (1994) *Managing the Mosaic: diversity in action*, London, CIPD.

Korac-Kakabadse, N., Kouzmin, A., Korac-Kakabadse, A. and Savery, L. (2001) Low- and High-context Communication Patterns: towards mapping cross-cultural encounters, *Cross Cultural Management – an International Journal*, 8 (2), 3–24.

Lewis, D. and Allan, B. (2004) *Virtual Learning Communities*, Maidenhead, Open University Press.

Pauleen, D. and Yoong, P. (2001) Facilitating Virtual Team Relationships via Internet and Conventional Communication Channels, *Internet Research: Electronic Networking Applications and Policy*, **11** (3), 190–202.

Pilling, S. and Kenna, S. (eds) (2002) *Co-operation in Action: collaborative initiatives in the world of information*, London, Facet Publishing.

Salmon, G. (2000) E-moderating, London, Kogan Page.

Schneider, S. C. and Barsoux, J. L. (1997) *Managing Across Cultures*, London, Prentice Hall.

Sullivan, H. and Skelcher, C. (2002) *Working Across Boundaries*, Basingstoke, Palgrave, Macmillan.

8 Human resource management

Introduction

As a team leader or supervisor you are likely to have contact with the human resources or personnel department when dealing with people issues. The purpose of this chapter is to provide an overview of the types of processes and activities that are involved in human resource management. This will help you to know and understand how the work of these specialists can support and help you in your work.

An important point to note is that if you are involved in a staff issue then it is always best to obtain expert advice from human resource specialists before attempting to tackle the problem. Employment legislation is constantly changing and developing, and this makes it imperative to ask for specialist assistance when dealing with staff issues.

The topics covered in this chapter are: human resource management, recruitment and selection, performance management and appraisal processes, disciplinary and grievance procedures, health and safety, managing absence, and equal opportunities and diversity. A useful and standard textbook on the subject is Torrington et al. (2005).

Human resource management

Large organizations will typically include a human resources department (previously called the personnel department) which is concerned with the strategic management of staff so that they support the goals and objectives of the organization. The human resources department is likely to take on the following responsibilities:

- administration of recruitment and selection
- servicing contracts of employment
- health and safety
- personnel policies and procedures
- supporting team leaders and managers in their dealings with their staff
- consultation with the recognized trade unions and other employee representatives
- workplace learning and development
- development and maintenance of personnel management systems

- provision of employment information, including statistics, for use within the organization and by related outside bodies
- presenting the organization's personnel policies and views in appropriate forums outside the organization.

Smaller organizations may employ one or two human resources officers and their function may be more narrowly focused on recruitment and selection, industrial relations, employment policies and practices, and health and safety.

Activity: Human resource management

How well do you know and understand human resource management in your organization? If you do not know and understand this process then it is worthwhile spending some time finding out about it, identifying who is responsible for different aspects of human resource management, and identifying relevant human resource policies and procedures. A good starting point is likely to be organizational documents, e.g. organizational structure, staff website, intranet site or portal, and your own manager.

Recruitment and selection

The purpose of recruitment and selection is to obtain staff with appropriate knowledge, skills and attitudes to enable the ILS to achieve its objectives. Most organizations provide specialist training to their supervisors, managers and leaders who are involved in the recruitment and selection process. If you are given the opportunity then it is worthwhile attending such events as they provide valuable information and assistance on this process.

There are three stages to this process: identifying the human resource requirements and gaining permission to go ahead and recruit new staff; attracting suitable candidates for the vacancy; filling the vacancy by selecting the most appropriate candidate. It is important throughout this process that you do not discriminate against individuals on the basis of age, gender, religion, cultural background, sexual orientation, disability, etc.

The recruitment and selection process may start as the result of someone leaving the ILS or being promoted within it, an increase in workload, the development of new services or products, or the identification of the need to expand the staff base. Whatever the reason someone, and this may be the team leader, must put forward a case to justify the recruitment of a new member of staff. Some organizations have a standard pro-forma that is used in this process. At this stage a detailed job description and person specification may need to be produced for the vacancy too.

Job description

A typical job description includes

- job title and department/unit
- the aims and purpose of the job
- the duties and responsibilities associated with the post
- the relationship to other jobs
- who the job holder is responsible to (the line manager's job title)
- who the job holder is responsible for (the job titles managed directly by the post holder)
- other key working relationships within the organization
- status of post (grade, salary, hours of work, whether permanent or fixed-term contract)
- any allowances that are attracted to the post (mileage, childcare).

Person specification

The person specification outlines the minimum qualifications and experience required to fulfil the role. These are likely to be divided into essential criteria and desirable criteria. The essential criteria may be used to identify those candidates who are able to do the job while the desirable criteria may be used to distinguish further where a large number of candidates may be eligible for shortlisting. It is important to make sure that the person specification complies with current legislation and it is advisable to take advice on this from your human resources department.

Advertising the post

Once permission has been received to fill the role then it will be advertised, e.g. via the internet, newspapers or professional literature. Some organizations use recruitment agencies, either general high-street agencies or specialist information and library services. Examples in the UK include INFORMATCH, TFPL Recruitment Ltd, ASLIB/IMI Recruitment Services and Sue Hill Recruitment and Services Ltd. It is likely that the human resources staff will lead this process because they will need to ensure that the documentation is compliant with legal and organizational policies. In addition, they will need to ensure that it conforms to equal opportunities legislation. Adverts typically contain the following information:

- organization's name, location and logo
- brief introduction to the organization or department
- job title
- status of post (whether full-time or part-time, permanent or fixed-term)
- salary and other rewards

- main purpose of job
- the essential criteria for the job
- how to get an application form and further details
- a closing date for applications
- information on how to obtain a copy of the advertisement and an application form in different formats.

Shortlisting

Once the applications have been received the team leader is likely to be involved in the shortlisting process. This involves checking each application against the person specification and using evidence from the application to support each decision. Candidates who do not meet all the essential characteristics listed in the person specification will be deleted from the pile of applications. The remaining candidates will then be scored and the top 6–12 candidates will be invited for interview. It is essential that this process is based on factual evidence recorded on the application and that a full record of all decisions and the reasons for each decision is kept. Unsuccessful candidates need to be written to and given the opportunity to gain feedback on their application. It is vitally important that recruitment and selection (and indeed all human resource management processes and activities) comply with relevant legislation. There are some people who make a career from applying for positions and then attempting to gain money by taking the organization to court on the basis of some transgression of equal opportunities or other legislation.

Case study 8.1   Shortlisting for library assistants

A number of years ago I was involved in shortlisting for five vacancies for library assistants. I worked with two colleagues and we had all undergone the university's recruitment and selection training process. We had over 100 applications and the first stage in the decision-making process involved identifying and rejecting candidates who did not fulfil the essential criteria. We quickly eliminated 50 applications. We then used a scoring system to assess and rank the remaining applications by checking their application against the essential and desirable criteria. We then interviewed the top 20 candidates and selected five people for the vacancies. Three team leaders carried out this process and we kept a careful record of all the decisions that we made and the rationale for our decision-making. The human resources department managed the whole procedure including informing candidates of the outcome of their applications.

One month later I received a phone call from the human resources department and was told that one of the unsuccessful candidates, who had not been shortlisted for an interview, had put in a formal claim via his solicitor that he had been discriminated against on the grounds of race. I was called to a meeting with the human resources department and the university's solicitors. I explained the procedure that we had gone through and supported it using the evidence from our records of our shortlisting meeting.

One of the essential criteria was 'Experience and use of common ICT packages, virtual learning environments such as Blackboard and WebCT, and use of specialist library software e.g. circulation systems'. I was able to illustrate from the documentation that this particular candidate had written 'I am experienced in using many computer packages' and not provided any other evidence to support his claim. From our perspective he had not demonstrated this essential criterion. Candidates who had demonstrated that they fulfilled this criterion had included the following types of comments in their applications:

> I am familiar with and have used Word, Excel, Access and PowerPoint. In addition, as a student I regularly used Blackboard. I have no practical experience of using specialist library software but I am willing to learn how to use it.
> I obtained the full European Driving Licence in 2005 and I am experienced in the use of Blackboard. I have also used the library system, ALICE, in my voluntary work in a school library.

This evidence enabled the university's solicitors and the human resources department to assess that the correct recruitment and selection procedures had been followed and they complied with equal opportunities legislation. They informed the unsuccessful candidate's lawyer of the outcomes of the meeting and no more was heard from him. From my perspective, this was an uncomfortable experience. However, it illustrates the value of training events on recruitment and selection, following all the appropriate procedures, and keeping a detailed record of the process and the decisions.

Interview

The human resources team may lead the interview process or it may be represented on the interview panel. Planning the interview process means ensuring that the relevant staff are available, making arrangements for the candidates to be met at reception or the ILS help desk, organizing a suitable waiting room and also refreshments. In addition, the panel members need to prepare in advance how they will test and measure each of the elements in the person specification. Whatever process they decide upon it is essential that each candidate is treated in exactly the same way and the process needs to be clearly recorded and documented. The actual interview process may involve a variety of activities, e.g. a traditional interview, a presentation, an in-tray exercise, a test, a group activity and interview. Practical tests may involve activities such as putting a shelf of books in order, a typing test, or an online search test. These are very good ways of testing the validity of claims in an application form. In addition, the candidates will be shown around the ILS and may be given the opportunity to meet with and talk to staff.

Most recruitment processes involve a traditional interview and these often have the following structure:

- beginning:
  — welcome
  — introductions – name, role, shake hands
  — creating rapport – talk about niceties, weather, travel, etc.
  — explanation of the interview procedure
  — summary of the job
- middle:
  — a series of pre-prepared questions
  — each question can be followed up by additional supplementary questions or discussion
  — one or more people are likely to make notes of the responses
- end:
  — opportunity for the candidate to ask questions
  — explanation about travel expenses, other details
  — explanation of how the candidate will be informed of the results of the interview
- thank you and good-byes.

Appointment

At the end of the interview process, a decision is made on the successful candidate. Many employers also identify the candidates who came second and third just in case the successful candidate doesn't accept the position. The decision must be based on evidence of how closely the candidates match the person specification. As with shortlisting, the process needs to be clearly documented just in case queries arise around the decision-making processes involved in the selection process, e.g. as a result of potential litigation.

After the decision has been made both the successful and unsuccessful candidates need to be contacted and informed of the result. For the successful candidate, the human resources department will need to organize the employment contract and provide the new recruit with an information pack relating to their new role in the organization. They will also organize the date on which the recruit will start work. On their first day the new recruit will enter an induction process.

Induction

An important responsibility for team leaders is the induction of new staff. The purpose of induction is to enable new recruits to settle into the workplace and to get to know the organization, their department and team, and their job role. If you are working in a large organization new members of staff may be asked to attend an induction programme provided for staff from a wide range of departments. This type of event will include a mixture of presentations and tours, e.g. I once worked as an information officer for a major construction company and my induction process included trips to quarries, a road-building operation and a house-building site. This type of induction event is useful as it provides the new recruit with valuable information about the organization as a whole. However, it may be scheduled several weeks or months after the starting date.

As team leader it is highly probable that you will be actively involved in developing and delivering the induction programme for new staff. When you are planning the induction process it is important to think about it in terms of what someone must know, and this may be structured in the following way:

First day

- introduction to key personnel:
  — introduction to team leader, team and other key members of staff
  — introduction to personal 'buddy'
- essential registration:
  — meet with human resource department staff to complete and obtain documents relating to pay, time sheets, annual leave, sickness absence, probationary period, etc.
  — obtain staff card
  — obtain computer access
- general:
  — introduction to work environment
  — overview of team and its work
  — outline arrangements regarding toilets, tea/coffee-making facilities, lockers, car parking, bicycle bays, etc.
  — tour of department and building
- health and safety:
  — fire and evacuation procedures
  — accident reporting procedures
  — location of first aiders
  — other emergency reporting procedures
  — hazard and fault reporting procedures
  — smoking policy
- work schedule:
  — outline schedule for week 1.

First week

- introduction to other key members of staff
- overview of department/organization and its work
- introduction to working arrangements:
  — post
  — photocopying

    — administration
    — stationery
    — telephone system
    — computer systems
    — notice boards
- introduction to relevant policies and procedures:
    — equal opportunities
    — diversity
    — disciplinary
    — capability
    — health and safety
    — race equality
    — disability
- provision of staff lists/contact details.

First six months

- identification of training needs
- planned training activities
- introduction and appropriate experience in different areas of activity in the department
- introduction and guides to different sites and specialist working areas
- introduction and familiarization with relevant departments in the organization.

A successful induction process

The first week is a critical stage in the induction of a new member of staff. At this stage people are frequently very anxious and this makes them less likely to remember key facts, e.g. names and working procedures. This means that it is worthwhile gently phasing in their induction process and not expecting people to remember too much in their first week of work. Sometimes a 'buddy' is allocated to look after a new member of staff and this provides them with someone, normally a member of their team, who is willing and able to respond to the many questions that arise as someone is settling into their new job.

To help new staff keep a track of and feel some ownership over their induction process many information and library services provide an induction checklist covering the points listed above. This enables the individual member of staff to feel some ownership and control over the process and it enables them to check off when each stage in the process has been completed. The checklist may be used as the basis of discussion between the team leader and the new recruit at regular stages in their induction process.

Performance management and appraisal

Performance management and appraisal systems are powerful tools that may be used to review, motivate, develop and retain staff. The main difference between the two systems is that performance management is directly linked to business objectives and is often linked to reward systems. However, some organizations use the two terms interchangeably so as team leader it is important to know how your organization manages and implements its performance management and appraisal system. Torrington et al. identify the characteristics of performance systems as:

- Top-down link between business objectives and individual objectives . . .
- Line manager driven and owned (rather than being owned by the human resource function . . .)
- A living document where performance plans, support and ongoing review are documented as work progresses, and prior to annual review . . .
- Performance is rewarded and reinforced.

Torrington et al. (2005, 263)

Some performance management systems are extremely formal and require the completion of lengthy documents by managers or supervisors and their staff. The 360° performance management process involves gaining feedback from a number of colleagues, and may require numerous documents to be completed. Some performance management schemes are linked with reward systems, e.g. staff may be scored during the process and those staff achieving a score above a certain level may be given a pay rise or bonus. For example, individuals may be rated using the following continuum:

1 consistently surpasses expectations
2 frequently exceeds expectations
3 consistently fulfils expectations
4 needs improvement to fully achieve expectations
5 fails to achieve expectations.

In contrast, an appraisal process involves the formal assessment of an individual's performance against specific targets, and then setting new targets to be achieved during the next appraisal process. This process normally involves a meeting between the team leader and the member of staff and it provides both parties with the opportunity to give and discuss feedback. Appraisal schemes normally run on an annual cycle. Appraisal systems are typically designed to:

- improve staff performance
- provide feedback on individual performance
- identify training needs
- consider individual career development.

Different organizations will structure and organize their appraisal processes in a manner that meets their needs. Some schemes are less formal and may require only the completion of one sheet of A4 paper by the team leader and member of staff.

A common feature of both performance management and appraisal meetings is the setting of objectives, covered in Chapter 5. Sometimes learning contracts are agreed during appraisal meetings and these are used as a means of agreeing learning and training plans with a member of staff. A learning contract is likely to include the following information and an example of a completed contract is given in Figure 8.1.

- name of staff member(s)
- aim of workplace learning plan
- learning outcomes
- proposed method(s) of delivery
- name of staff supporting the workplace learning activity
- timescale
- assessment activities
- evaluation process.

Name of staff member(s)	Ibrahim Abdallh
Aim of training plan	To enable Ibrahim to develop his skills in information searching for business information.
Learning outcomes	By the end of July, Ibrahim will be able to: identify and explain the characteristics of the main electronic sources of business information carry out an advanced search on the main databases evaluate the results of the searches.
Proposed method(s) of delivery	Work through open learning package. Shadow Sam, practise by self. Use information from open learning package, talk to Sam. Visit Business Information Service in Public Library.
Name of staff supporting the workplace learning activity	Sam will act as a buddy.
Timescale	To be completed by 31 July.
Assessment activities	Ibrahim will provide an introduction to electronic business sources at the team meeting in August.
Evaluation process	Ibrahim to provide feedback on standard form by end of July.
Agreed by	Ibrahim Abdallh (Information Officer) Anne Jones (Team Leader)

Figure 8.1 Sample learning contract

Part of the role of a team leader or supervisor is to lead performance or appraisal review meetings. If you are asked to lead such a meeting then it is vital to attend any training session provided by your organization because this will help you to prepare for these meetings and also give you confidence in running the meetings. Preparation and management of these meetings is likely to involve the following issues (adapted from appraisal guidance outlines produced by the University of Hull).

What is an appraisal review and how frequent should it be?

- It is an opportunity for a member of staff to have a one-to-one discussion with their team leader or supervisor.
- The discussion will be based around performance at work over the period since the last review and targets for future performance will be agreed.
- It should also identify workplace learning activities which will support the achievement of these targets.
- A review provides staff with constructive feedback about their contribution to the success of the organization.
- A review should be conducted annually with a six-monthly revisit recommended.

What is not included in a review?

- Discussions relating to pay.
- Any issue which may lead to disciplinary action – this should be addressed at the time it occurs and not mentioned during a review.

How should you organize a review meeting?

- Agree a convenient date and time with the member of staff – this should be during working hours and at a time when neither of you will be called away.
- Find a suitable location in a comfortable area where you will not be disturbed.
- Give yourself time to prepare for the review:
  — Think about the individual's performance at work.
  — Look back at the last review you did with them.
  — Have they achieved the targets you agreed at that time?
  — Have the training activities you agreed been completed?
  — Thought should be given to examples of when the staff member has demonstrated the required competencies and their overall achievements.
- The review is a two-way process: both staff member and team leader are expected to prepare effectively for the review meeting. Both parties should have a copy of the last review and a blank copy of the review document.

How should the review be conducted?

- Help the team member to feel relaxed. Start by explaining the process.
- Don't do all the talking! You must give the member of staff the opportunity to talk to you about how they feel they have performed before you add your own comments.
- Relax! This is meant to be a comfortable and relatively informal discussion.
- Be honest and open – if you are discussing an area in which the member of staff has not performed as well as they could, be *constructive not critical*.
- Always give your member of staff the chance to ask questions or make general comments.

How do I use and complete the review form?

- The most important thing about a review is that all staff have the opportunity to have a one-to-one discussion with their team leader. The review document should be completed after the meeting as it provides a record for the future.
- You may prefer to take notes during your discussion and complete the document afterwards. This should be within five working days of the review meeting.

Disciplinary policy and procedures

Unfortunately, problems sometimes arise with individuals in the workplace and a disciplinary process may need to take place. Disciplining staff is an unpleasant activity but it is actually essential to the well-being of the organization. Individuals who behave in an unacceptable manner, e.g. bullying and harassment of other staff, or theft of organizational resources, damage the team, the department and the organization as a whole. In some circumstances the employer could be liable for damages for breach of contract. This means that disciplinary procedures should be used where necessary. As part of the recruitment process, new employees will receive a copy of the disciplinary code and the consequent disciplinary procedures for breaking it.

If you are a team leader or supervisor who thinks that there is a disciplinary issue then it is vital to obtain specialist advice from the human resources specialists BEFORE you take either informal or formal action. Without this advice you may find yourself on the receiving end of an allegation of harassment or bullying.

Disciplinary codes normally outline the organization's approach to discipline and also the involvement of trade unions. Most codes aim at enabling the issue to be dealt with through an informal meeting between the supervisor and member of staff. The purpose of the informal meeting is to attempt to identify the nature of the problem, its causes and possible solutions. The result of this informal meeting is normally an action plan which should be agreed in writing by both parties in an attempt to resolve matters. Most organizations' disciplinary codes enable the staff member to be accompanied by their trade union representative or a work colleague.

The team leader needs to advise the member of staff that if there is no improvement the next stage will be the formal disciplinary procedure. The supervisor is advised to keep a record of the informal discussion. If the matter is not resolved then it will move into a formal procedure. Formal disciplinary procedures are normally managed and led by the human resources team who know that if they don't comply with their written formal procedures then they may end up in a tricky and possibly litigious situation.

Formal procedures normally involve a verbal warning, a first written warning, a final written warning and then dismissal.

Most organizations dismiss staff who are found guilty of gross misconduct and this involves staff who have been involved in:

- assault or physical violence
- theft, fraud, falsifying time-sheets or other records
- misuse of information communications technology, e.g. via e-mail or the internet
- serious breaches of regulations relating to health and safety or data protection
- serious breaches of the organization's policies relating to equal opportunities, diversity and bullying and harassment
- any other serious issue of misconduct or issue of negligence where the organization reasonably believes that the actual or potential consequences are extremely serious or where the reputation of the organization is or could be seriously damaged.

Case study 8.2   Running a business

A team leader, Janet, working within an academic library became aware that one of her team members, Charles, regularly made mobile phone calls in the car park during his breaks and he often had visits from students which didn't fit in with his job role of accessions assistant. She was puzzled by this set of circumstances but didn't take any action. One day a new library assistant, Raphael, came to her and said that he had been asked to hand over packages at the library counter and receive money from the students which he was supposed to put in a little red box in the workroom. He thought that this was sloppy practice and that the money should be recorded and the student given a proper receipt. Janet thanked this member of staff for his feedback and asked him to e-mail it to her. She then called a team meeting and asked her team to clarify what was happening. At the meeting nobody said anything but afterwards someone phoned her and explained that Charles was running a second-hand book business via the internet and using the library as his distribution centre. Janet immediately contacted the human resources department who took over the management of the issue. The outcome of the case was a disciplinary hearing; Charles attended supported by his union representative. Janet was asked to attend too and she outlined the situation from her perspective. The outcome of the case was that Charles received a final warning. The next day Janet met Charles in the car park and he said to her 'It was a fair cop.' One month later he resigned from his post and is still running his book business.

Grievance policy and procedures

The purpose of a grievance procedure is to enable members of staff to raise issues with their employer about their work or about their manager's or colleagues' actions that affect them. Examples of issues raised in grievance procedures include equal opportunities issues; perceived unreasonable requests by a manager or colleagues; and perceived unfair treatment in working practices. Most organizations provide training for team leaders and managers so that they have the necessary knowledge, skills and experience to operate the grievance policy and procedures effectively. This is vital if the organization and the individual team leader are not to find themselves in front of an industrial tribunal.

In the UK an organization's grievance procedures are designed to comply with the government's statutory grievance procedure. If a member of your team wishes to raise a grievance it is important to contact the human resources department and read the relevant grievance policy and procedures. Normally grievances must be put in writing and individuals with a grievance have the right to support from a trade union representative or a work colleague. Individual grievance procedures vary but they normally include an informal stage where the member(s) of staff and their line manager or team leader attempt to resolve the issue through an informal discussion and action plan. If this doesn't resolve the issue the grievance may move to the formal stages. Typically this involves a first formal meeting between the member(s) of staff and their line manager and, if this doesn't resolve the problem, then it would involve a second formal meeting and at this stage a human resources manager or organizational director may be involved in the meeting. If this doesn't resolve the issue or if the member of staff is dissatisfied with the outcome they can enter an appeal process. The formal grievance procedure outlines the detail which structures how these meetings should be organized, the timeline of the process and also the ways in which the process must be communicated to interested parties and also documented.

Health and safety at work

Health and safety at work is about preventing people from being harmed at work by taking the right precautions and providing a satisfactory work environment. In the UK legislation covering health and safety at work includes:

- Health and Safety at Work Act 1974
- Management of Health and Safety at Work Regulations 1992
- Health and Safety (Consultation with Employees) Regulations 1996
- Safety Representatives and Safety Committees Regulations 1977.

In the UK the Health and Safety Executive (HSE) and local authorities administer these laws. You can find out more about health and safety at work by contacting your health and safety officer or the HSE at www.hse.gov.uk.

There are many common risks at work and typical examples relevant to information and library work include slips, trips and falls; hazardous substances; lifting and carrying; repetitive movements; noise; work equipment. Other hazards include vibration; electricity; maintenance and building work; fire, explosion or radiation. One of the roles of the team leader or supervisor is to provide a lead on health and safety within their team. This is likely to involve liaising with the organization's health and safety officers, attending relevant training courses and ensuring that you, your team and customers all comply with health and safety requirements. Health and safety legislation and requirements are constantly changing so it is essential to keep up to date, e.g. by reading all memos and letters from health and safety officers and also attending all relevant courses.

Case study 8.3   Health and safety during a library move

I was involved in moving an academic library into a new building. In addition to the permanent staff, 17 temporary 'movers and shifters' were employed to carry out much of the manual work. Just before the move began all the permanent staff were given a refresher course on lifting and moving by the health and safety officer. On their first day of employment in the library all the temporary staff were given a half-day course on lifting and moving, and the university's health and safety officer also ran this course. These courses were carefully documented and everyone was expected to sign an attendance sheet both at the start and end of the course. The project team retained copies of the course outline and all teaching materials. On the second day of employment one of the temporary staff damaged his foot and, as a result, attempted to sue the university. After a long-drawn-out process which was managed by the university's solicitor the case was dropped because the project manager and university were able to demonstrate that they had taken appropriate action, which was well documented through the training course, to inform both temporary and permanent staff on good practice in manual handling and that the person in question had 'broken the rules'.

Activity: Health and safety

How well do you know and understand health and safety in your organization and department? If you do not know and understand how health and safety is managed within your organization then it is worthwhile spending some time finding out about it, identifying who is responsible for different aspects of health and safety, and identifying relevant policies and procedures. A good starting point is likely to be organizational documents, e.g. organizational structure, staff website, intranet site or portal, and your own manager.

Handling absenteeism

Absenteeism is often a major cause of concern for employers because people who are absent from work are unable to undertake their duties. This means that they either don't get done or other staff take on an additional burden. In addition, customer services may suffer. Reducing absenteeism is an important feature of human resources management. Typically human resource departments tackle absence by the following process:

- assess the absence problem
- locate the absence problem
- identify and prioritize the absence problem
- evaluate the current absence control methods
- design the absence control programme
- implement the absence control programme
- monitor the effectiveness of the absence control programme.

(Torrington et al., 2005, 324)

The sickness reporting process within an organization provides information that is used in the absence control programme. The human resources department is likely to contact the individual team leader or supervisor when someone's absence pattern over a period of time, e.g. six months or a year, triggers action. This report may be triggered due to the number of days off sick or the overall pattern of sickness such as regular absences on a particular day of the week. It triggers an absence review meeting where the team leader reviews the individual's absence record and works with them to enable them to improve their record. As with other human resource activities, the team leader normally receives special training in running this type of meeting and is provided with advice on the type of action that may be taken. This is important, as absence is often an indication of a complex range of factors causing pressure on an individual member of staff. Sometimes the solution to the issue may be developed in discussions with the team member, an occupational health specialist and a human resources officer.

Staff who have been away from work for some time, e.g. a month, may have a phased return to work and this is likely to be organized by the human resources department in collaboration with the person's team leader or supervisor. Back-to-work interviews are now commonly used as part of an absence control programme and these involve the team leader meeting with the member of staff when they return from work after an absence. These interviews may be held for someone who has been absent for a day, a week, or longer, depending on the policies and practices of the organization. The tone of discussions in these meetings is normally sympathetic and supportive, and may cover some or all of the following:

- reasons for the absence, including any contributory work, domestic or other 'non sickness' factors

- discussion of whether the absence is likely to reoccur and if there are any residual health problems
- update on any workplace developments that may have occurred during the absence period, e.g. how their work has been covered during their absence
- support or sources of further advice including any support for easing back into work
- if appropriate, a review of the absence record including any emerging patterns, e.g. regular Friday or Monday absence
- if appropriate, agreement on an action plan arising from the discussion. This will be discussed with the human resources department after the meeting and, if necessary, may include a referral to an occupational health practitioner.

Equal opportunities and diversity policies and practices

The concept of equal opportunities developed during the 1970s and 1980s and it is based around a view of the rights of the individual to universally applicable standards of justice and citizenship. This approach is underpinned by the concept that everyone should have equal access to organizations and services, e.g. education and health services, and rewards, e.g. pay and pensions irrespective of gender, race, ethnicity or sexual orientation. In the UK this approach is underpinned by legislation such as the Equal Pay Act 1970, Sex Discrimination Act 1975, Race Relations Act 1976 and the Trade Union and Labour Relations (Consolidation) Act 1992, and by legislation introduced in the European Union such as the Equality (Sexual Orientation) Regulations 2003, the Employment Equality (Religion and Belief) Regulations 2003, and the Age Discrimination Act 2006. A useful source of up-to-date information and guidance in the UK is the Equal Opportunities Commission website (www.eoc.org.uk). In the workplace, personnel or human resources departments are concerned with developing, implementing and monitoring policies and procedures to ensure compliance with this legislation. Organizational strategies used to support an equal opportunities approach include policy statements, inequality-proof recruitment and selection procedures, monitoring, special courses to support specific groups, e.g. IT skills for women, family-friendly policies, improved access for people with disabilities, harassment and bullying policies and procedures.

In the 1990s the equal opportunities agenda shifted to become a model of diversity and this shift is located within an organizational environment that involves a move towards deregulation, flexibility, new managerialism, human resource management, internationalism and globalization. The shift from equal opportunities to managing diversity has been presented in a number of different ways: as an evolutionary step; a sophistication of the equal opportunities approach; repackaging of equal opportunities; a market driven notion; or as an approach to allow employers to avoid working against discrimination (Kirton and Greene, 2000). A commonly used definition of diversity is presented in Chapter 7 and is repeated here:

The basic concept of managing diversity accepts the workforce consists of a diverse population of people. The diversity consists of visible and non-visible differences which will include factors such as sex, age, background, race, disability and work style. It is founded on the premise that harnessing these differences will create a productive environment in which everyone feels valued, where their talents are being fully utilised and their organisational goals are met.

Kandola and Fullerton (1994, 8)

This definition links a number of different ideas: that organizations should recognize differences, that these differences are a strength and that they may be utilized to benefit the organization. An example of legislation that underpins this approach is the Disability Discrimination Act 1995. Examples of interventions based on this model include diversity training, provision of support programmes, e.g. mentoring for aspiring women managers, and approaches that focus on individual differences rather than differences based on a relatively small number of group characteristics such as race or gender.

What are the differences between equal opportunities and managing diversity? Torrington et al. (2005) provide a useful summary of the major differences and this is presented in Table 8.1. There are some similarities between the two approaches and how they may be enacted within an organization. However, there are some important differences. Managing diversity involves maximizing potential rather than focusing on the prevention of discrimination and fear of possible litigation. Managing diversity involves a broader range of people than that traditionally dealt with under equal opportunities legislation and policies. Managing diversity recognizes individuality rather than groups. A useful discussion on the debate concerning equal opportunities and managing diversity is presented by Torrington et al. (2005).

What does it mean in practice? Individual team leaders and supervisors need to read and understand their organization's equal opportunities and diversity policies and practices. Most organizations run training sessions for new supervisors and team

Table 8.1   Differences between equal opportunities and managing diversity
Note: adapted from Torrington et al. (2005)

Aspect	Equal opportunities	Managing diversity
Purpose	Reduce discrimination	Utilize the potential of all employees to enable the organization to achieve its objectives
Rationale	Moral and ethical	Business case
Responsibility	Human resources department	All team leaders and managers
Focuses on	Groups	Individuals
Benefits for employees	Opportunities improved for members of disadvantaged groups	Opportunities improved for everyone
Organizational approach	Policies and procedures	Culture

leaders to help them understand the topic of equal opportunities and managing diversity, and to draw out the implications of the legislation for workplace practices. The most important aspect of this subject is to be aware of equal opportunities and diversity, and to bear it in mind on a day-to-day basis. If in doubt then contact your human resources department.

Summary

Specialists in human resource management are employed by organizations to help ensure that they have staff that are willing and able to achieve the organization's objectives. These specialist staff are there to help and support team leaders and supervisors in areas such as recruitment and selection, performance management and appraisal processes, disciplinary and grievance procedures, health and safety, managing absence, and equal opportunities and diversity. The main message from this chapter is that it is vitally important to ask for and use specialist support and advice when dealing with many people issues. The alternative is to risk ending up in front of an industrial tribunal or court.

References

Kandola, R. and Fullerton, J. (1994) *Managing the Mosaic: diversity in action*, London, CIPD.

Kirton, G. and Greene, A.-M. (2000) *The Dynamics of Managing Diversity*, Oxford, Elsevier Butterworth-Heinemann.

Torrington, D., Hall, L. and Taylor, S. (2005) *Human Resource Management*, 6th edn, London, Prentice Hall.

9   Workplace learning and training

Introduction

This chapter outlines approaches to managing workplace learning, and then identifies and explains the planned workplace learning cycle. This cycle may be used to implement any type of workplace learning activities, e.g. coaching sessions, demonstrations, training events. This is followed by an in-depth discussion of different types of workplace learning activities including e-learning, coaching, and learning through reflection.

Context of workplace learning

Team leaders in the 21st century face many challenges including the need to ensure that their team has the knowledge and skills required to produce high-quality work. We are working in a rapidly changing environment – one that is characterized by accelerating change, continuing information explosion and continuing changes to communication and information technologies. In addition, new approaches to living, working and learning as illustrated by the shift to a 24/7 society, the development of a mobile and global workforce, and the expansion of learning from traditional places such as schools, colleges and universities into the community and workplace have provided further challenges for information and library services.

In recent years there has been a shift in emphasis from the idea of training and development to the concept of lifelong learning and continuous professional development (CPD). What is training and how is it distinguished from concepts such as development, continuous or continuing professional development and lifelong learning? In practice, people often use these words interchangeably:

* **Training**. Often used to refer to learning that is associated with the development of very specific skills and behaviours that are required in the workplace. Training may take place through a wide range of activities, e.g. through instruction, coaching, on-the-job training and e-learning. It frequently involves attending specific training events organized by the employing organization or a professional association such as CILIP.
* **Development**. A broader term including all types of learning that are associated with personal and career development; these may or may not be work-related. It takes place through gaining a variety of work experience,

attendance on education and training programmes, e.g. university or college-based degree or diploma, and workplace activities such as mentoring.

* **Continuous or continuing professional development (CPD)**. Relates to the idea that learning and development is an ongoing process and essential for individuals involved in any kind of professional practice. The concept often includes the idea of a 'reflective practitioner', i.e. someone who thinks about and reflects upon their professional work and uses their reflections as the basis for professional development. CPD is often discussed in terms of it being the responsibility of the individual practitioner. It is supported by professional associations such as CILIP and encompasses a broad range of learning and development activities ranging from individual reflection through to engagement with education and training programmes.
* **Lifelong learning**. A concept that is widely used to underpin educational policies and theories. Many international bodies, e.g. UNESCO, EU and OECD, have highlighted the need for lifelong learning as a response to economic, political, social and technological changes (Kreber, 2005). Fundamentally the concept is concerned with the idea that individuals need to develop their knowledge and skills throughout their lifetime in order to play an active role in society, e.g. through employment or other activities.

In this chapter the focus is on workplace learning, which includes a wide range of learning activities including training events. There are many different ways in which individuals and teams can learn in the workplace. Examples are listed in Figure 9.1.

Analysing mistakes	Demonstrating	Meetings	Research
Appraisals	Dialogue/discussion	Mentoring	Reviewing learning
Asking and answering questions	E-learning	Multimedia resources	Rotating jobs
	E-mail	Networking	Secondments
Asking for advice	Exhibitions	Newsletters	Self-assessment questionnaires
Audio tapes	Feedback	Open learning packages	
Cascade training	FAQ	Organizing an event	Self-development books
Changing jobs	Individual projects	Praising	Shadowing
Coaching	Induction programmes	Presentations	Teamwork
Computer-based training	Internet	Producing guides	Training videos
	Job exchanges	Project work	Visits
Covering for holiday	Learning contracts	Quizzes	Vocational qualifications
Crises	Learning logs	Reading	Weblogs
Debriefing	Listening	Reflection	
Delegation	Manuals	Rehearsing	

Figure 9.1 Potential learning activities in the workplace

Management of workplace learning

Workplace learning, training and development are the responsibility of an organization. If you work in a large organization you will need to understand how it is managed. At a strategic level, senior managers will produce a training and development strategy which is a strategic document that outlines the overall direction and aims of staff training and development. An example of the contents of this type of document is given in Figure 9.2.

Aim of staff training and development within the organization.
Who is responsible for staff training and development.
Who is eligible for training.
The process for identifying training needs.
What types of training are available and on what basis.
Guidelines for access to training and development.
The balance between work-based learning and off-the-job training.
Forms of learning/learning outcomes favoured.
The process for applying and attending training.
Appeal process for decisions related to training.

Figure 9.2 Training and development strategy – outline structure

The process of workplace learning, training and development is likely to be managed at an operational level by a human resources or personnel department. There may be one or more staff with a responsibility for this area and it is important for team leaders to understand how staff training and development are managed in their organization. This will help you to access appropriate and relevant activities. Many organizations produce a regular programme of events aimed at individuals and teams. In addition, the staff development officer or team should be willing to provide tailor-made events and activities for individual team leaders and managers.

Large information and library services are likely to provide their own staff workplace development process which often mirrors the organizational one. For example the ILS may have its own workplace learning, training and development strategy; a member of staff may have a special responsibility for workplace learning, training and development activities, and they may produce their own programme of events.

Individuals leading teams in small information and library units, e.g. in the workplace or in voluntary organizations, may find that they have relatively little support or understanding of their learning and development needs from their parent organization or management. In this case, team leaders must plan and design the workplace learning processes themselves.

Workplace learning cycle

The workplace learning cycle is fundamentally the same if you are working in a large organization or in a small one, and it involves four stages: needs analysis; plan and design; delivery; evaluation. This cycle is described in Figure 9.3 and working through it enables team leaders to ensure that the workplace learning and training provided is:

- relevant to the needs of the organization, ILS, team and individual
- appropriately designed and delivered
- evaluated to ensure continuous improvement.

The stages in the workplace learning cycle are outlined below.

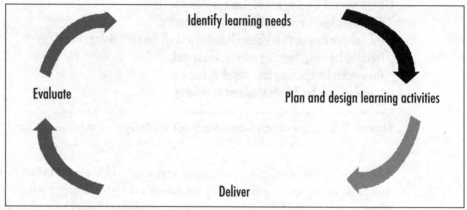

Figure 9.3 The workplace learning cycle

Identifying learning needs

Common triggers that cause team leaders to think about learning needs include the appointment of new staff or promotion of existing staff, the desire to improve performance, critical incidents such as complaints from customers, or the introduction of new systems or services. Learning needs arise as a result of three main types of activity within the ILS: identifying the gap between present and desired performance; improving performance to achieve continually rising standards; and innovating, i.e. doing new and better things. This is illustrated in Case study 9.1.

Case study 9.1   Identifying training needs
Identifying the gap

Clare was the team leader of two staff who worked as information skills trainers in a large academic library. She noticed that Jane, one of the trainers, consistently received poor feedback on the training evaluation forms. The feedback from students stated that her sessions were boring although they also stated that Jane was extremely knowledgeable about information sources in their subject. Jane and Clare discussed this performance gap and decided that it could be met through a range of workplace learning and training activities.

Improving performance

In the same team of trainers, John identified that he would like to improve his skills in teaching large groups of students. Although he received positive feedback from his sessions he was convinced he could improve them. He discussed his performance with his team leader, Clare, and they agreed that it could be enhanced through a range of workplace learning and training activities.

Innovating

Clare and her team wished to expand their use of e-learning in the teaching of information skills. They particularly wanted to get involved in assessment activities such as diagnostic testing and end-of-course testing for students. They decided that in order to develop new approaches to e-learning they would need to develop their knowledge and skills about assessment and the use of test facilities in a virtual environment.

Specifying learning needs

This involves identifying the required knowledge, skills and attitudes needed by individual members of staff or the team as a whole. Specifying learning needs requires research and may involve the team leader:

- talking to team members and other colleagues
- looking at documents, e.g. appraisal documents, performance indicators or existing surveys
- observing the performance of team members
- benchmarking, i.e. visiting other teams, departments or information services to learn from their experiences.

The results of this process of specifying learning needs is a list of the learning outcomes that need to be achieved by individuals and/or the whole team. Learning outcomes are explained in more detail later in this chapter.

Planning and designing learning activities

Planning the learning activities involves deciding who, what, how, where and when they will take place. It involves producing a workplace learning plan that needs to be aligned with the LIS's business plans, departmental and/or unit objectives, team objectives and individual objectives. A simple example of a workplace learning plan is given in Figure 9.4. More detailed plans are produced for the whole ILS or organization and these are likely to identify the aim(s), rationale and link with ILS objectives, learning objectives/outcomes, skills and knowledge to be developed, workplace learning methods, numbers to be trained, duration of training, resource requirements and anticipated costs.

Information skills team Workplace learning plan 2007			
Name	Learning outcome	Learning and training activities	To be completed by
Clare	To improve her skills in project management	Read a book on project management. Attend a workshop on project management.	February 2007 April 2007
Jane	To use a wider range of training skills	Attend a one-day workshop run by CILIP. Observe one of John's sessions.	April 2007 February 2007
John	To use new approaches in teaching large groups	Attend a one-day workshop run by the university. Observe two or three lectures presented by staff known to be innovative in their approaches to teaching large groups.	April 2007 March 2007
Whole team	To use e-learning assessment tools in the information skills workshops	Invite a member of the e-learning team to give them an overview of the online assessment tools. Attend a workshop for support staff on assessing student learning.	February 2007 May 2007

Figure 9.4 Sample workplace learning plan

Once you have produced a training and development plan you need to spend some time designing individual workplace learning and teaching sessions or activities. Well-designed training and learning activities

- give you confidence so that you won't dry up
- focus your thinking on the needs of the learner
- help you to be prepared with appropriate learning materials
- help you to anticipate possible problems and develop contingency plans
- enable you to think through the whole event and take into account the principles of effective learning

- mean you are less likely to make basic errors during the training event or activity
- look professional.

The design process enables you to work out the learning process in detail, i.e. the overall structure of the event, content and sequence of all the activities that will enable you to meet the aim and objectives/outcomes of the training. There is no simple solution or prescription to designing effective training sessions. Successful training activities or sessions are those that are planned to meet organizational and individual learning needs and this involves setting realistic objectives that win learners' commitment. This involves thinking about the needs of individual learners, using a variety of learning activities, and making sure that they take place in an appropriate setting and, in particular, one that is away from distractions such as phones and e-mails.

The following guidelines are relevant to the design of a whole range of workplace learning activities including one-to-one training and coaching sessions, group sessions and presentations. It is crucial to the success of the training activity or programme to identify its purpose and what will be achieved. This will enable you to plan an appropriate session and then evaluate it afterwards. There are a number of ways in which this can be expressed:

- *Aims*. These are a broad statement of what the learning or training event aims to achieve. The aims will answer questions such as:
  — What is the purpose of this training event?
  — What is the event intended to achieve?

  Example: The aim of this session is to enable learners to learn the basic functions of a word-processing package.

- *Learning outcomes*. This is another way of specifying what someone will gain from the course. It is important to specify the learning outcomes accurately.

  Example: By the end of the course, learners will be able to:

  1. create, save and print a MS Word document
  2. use the standard formatting gestures on MS Word
  3. edit their document using tools such as Spellchecker
  4. insert and edit a basic table
  5. set up and use templates.

Outcomes must describe things that you are able to demonstrate that learners have learned. It is therefore helpful to avoid the use of words that describe non-observable states of mind. The following list of words is useful in compiling learning outcomes:

Analyse	Describe	List
Apply	Distinguish between	Outline
Assess	Evaluate	Prepare
Compare	Explain	State
Create	Give examples of	Suggest reasons why
Demonstrate	Identify	Summarize

The result of the design process is a detailed outline for each workplace learning event or activity. It is likely to contain the following information:

- title
- session aims/learning outcomes
- content – what you will be covering in the session
- delivery methods – mini-presentations, hands-on session, activities, use of CDs or DVDs, or e-learning
- assessment methods (informal or formal) such as observation, questioning, exercises or other activities
- learning materials and visual aids such as PowerPoint, e-learning training materials
- timetable for the event with the approximate timing of each activity
- outline of each activity
- details of the evaluation process.

An example of a completed outline is given in Figure 9.5. This example provides an outline of a session that could be used to introduce a group of staff to a customer-care policy.

Delivery

Chapter 6 provides guidance on presentation skills. Delivering the training event involves rigorous preparation; starting your session in an enthusiastic manner; providing an appropriate learning environment; working with people in a positive manner; observing the session; and remaining flexible.

- Preparation:
  — Make sure you have organized an appropriate training room or space.
  — Organize the team so that there will be no interruptions.
  — Make sure you have the relevant training resources and your session plan.
  — Take along a box of useful items, e.g. spare paper and pens, flipchart paper and pens, Blu-tak™, Post-it™ notes.
- Starting your session:
  — Look relaxed and well prepared.
  — Welcome everyone to the event.

Title: Introduction to customer relationship management						
Aim(s) The purpose of the session is to introduce the customer care policy to new members of staff						
Learning outcomes By the end of the session, staff will be able to: 1 explain the importance of customer care 2 outline the contents of the customer-care policy.						
Timing	Topic	Trainer activity	Learner	Assessment	Resources	Learning outcomes
	Health and safety	Before the start of the session check room and complete a risk assessment	N/a	N/a	N/a	
5 min.	Introductions	Introduce self, housekeeping arrangements. Introduce topic of day. Ask everyone to introduce themselves and say what they want from the session.	Listen. Introduce self and their learning objectives	N/a	Flipchart if group size >4	
5 min.	Why is customer care important?	Explain importance of customer care. Discuss what happens without good quality customer care. Use examples from shops, hotels.	Listen and discuss.	Observation	PowerPoint presentation	1
20 min.	What is the customer care policy?	Hand-out and explain the customer-care policy. Ask staff to produce a poster that outlines its key features.	Listen. Produce poster.	Observation	PowerPoint presentation, copies of customer-care policy, blank flipchart, paper and pens	2 2
8 min. 2 min.	QandA Close	Lead question and answer session. Thank staff for attending. Close session.	Discussion			

Figure 9.5 Example of a session outline for a 40-minute training activity

      — Start enthusiastically and with energy.
      — Get people involved.
      — Grab people's interest.
    • Provide an appropriate learning environment:
      — Provide a relaxed environment.
      — Enable the learners to feel comfortable and safe.
      — Provide the right level of challenge.
      — Make it interesting and fun.

- Work with people in a positive manner:
  — Give praise and constructive feedback.
  — Use positive language.
  — Don't dwell on errors or mistakes.
  — Turn negatives into positives.
- Observe the session:
  — Notice the energy level of the group (low, medium, high).
  — Notice the energy levels of trainer (low, medium, high).
  — Notice the levels of interest in the training material (low, medium, high).
  — Notice the level of humour in the group (low, medium, high).
  — Notice the focus of attention of individuals (self, others, trainer, training materials, elsewhere).
  — Notice participation levels in group discussions or exercises (low, medium, high).
- Be flexible:
  — Feel comfortable about responding to individual requests.
  — If you finish early then end the session – don't drag it out.
  — Let people speak and become involved in the session – even if it means you take minor detours from your plan.

Assessment

An important part of any training activity or event is assessment, that is the process of making a judgement based on evidence. In this chapter we are concerned with assessment as part of the workplace learning process rather than assessment as part of a certification process, e.g. towards a vocational or academic qualification. Why do we assess the impact of a workplace learning activity? Team leaders and trainers are constantly assessing their learners and this often takes place informally. The reasons for this assessment are to help support individual learning, to provide feedback to the learner and to provide feedback to the trainer or facilitator so that they can improve their practice. The assessment can take many forms. It can identify:

- what the learner knows or can do (e.g. at the start of the workplace learning activity)
- what the learner is learning (e.g. during the workplace learning activity)
- what the learner has learnt (e.g. by the end of the workplace learning activity)
- whether or not the learner has achieved the workplace learning activity objectives/learning outcomes.

The assessment process involves:

- identifying the criteria for assessment
- collecting the evidence from the learner(s), their peer(s) or their manager(s)
- making a judgement by comparing the evidence with the criteria
- giving feedback to the learner.

This is illustrated in Figure 9.6 which gives the example of the assessment of learning from a learning activity where a team leader is training a new member of staff to use a self-service loan machine.

In the context of team leaders leading and delivering training events and activities it is likely that much of the assessment process is informal and is carried out by observation and talking to the learner. Sometimes assessment is carried out using simple questionnaires to assess someone's knowledge and skill in using Microsoft Word (see Figure 9.7 on next page).

Assessment in a workplace learning activity to train a new member of staff in the use of a self-service loan machine	
1 Identifying the criteria for assessment	The team leader, in their role as trainer, will know the knowledge and skills needed to use the equipment correctly. If necessary they will check these in the equipment manual.
2 Workplace learning activity	The team leader will explain and demonstrate the equipment to the member of staff and give them a few opportunities to practise using it.
3 Collecting the evidence from the learner(s), their peer(s) or their manager(s)	The team leader will then give the learner the opportunity to demonstrate their knowledge and skill with the equipment, e.g. by explaining and demonstrating how to use it to the team leader or another person.
4 Making a judgement by comparing the evidence with the criteria	At this stage the team leader will make a judgement by comparing the individual's performance with the criteria for correctly using the machine.
5 Giving feedback to the learner	Constructive feedback is given on performance (see later in this chapter).

Figure 9.6 Assessment of learning from a workplace learning activity

The purpose of this feedback sheet is to help us to identify your training needs. Please rate your skills in the following areas:			
Use of MS Word facilities	Never used it	Hesitant use of feature	Confident user
Use of italics			
Use of tab			
Insert page numbers			
Insert a table			
Insert a chart from Excel			
Change margins			
Use footnotes			
Insert page numbers			
Use table of contents			
Use autoformat			
Use templates			

Figure 9.7 Sample IT skills inventory

Evaluation

The purpose of evaluating workplace learning activities is to obtain feedback about the success of the event or activity. Evaluation takes place in a number of different ways, e.g. evaluating individual reactions to the event, evaluating what people have learnt, evaluating the impact on individuals in the workplace and, finally, evaluating the impact on the service. The majority of organizations have standard evaluation processes for their workplace learning, training and development activities.

If you are working with individuals or your team using workplace training activities then a quick and easy way of evaluating them is to ask them to answer the following questions:

- What did you like?
- What could be improved?
- What did you learn?
- What will you do differently as a result of this learning activity?

Practical ways of asking these questions include writing them in a table, e.g. on flipchart paper, a Post-it™ note, or sheet of A4, and asking people to answer the questions either individually or in small groups (see Figure 9.8). You will notice that this set of questions has the same structure used in earlier chapters. Using a consistent approach to asking staff to evaluate or reflect on something is useful as the process soon becomes internalized and part of everyday practice.

What you liked	What could be improved
What you learnt	What will you do differently as a result of this learning activity?

Figure 9.8 Sample evaluation form

E-learning

In recent years there has been an explosive growth in e-learning and its use throughout the information world. Robin Mason (2002) describes three forms of e-learning: web-based training, supported online learning and informal e-learning. Table 9.1 summarizes the key characteristics of these approaches. This section focuses on two approaches to e-learning: web-based interactive learning packages and supported e-learning involving the use of communication technologies such as discussion groups and conference rooms to support collaborative learning in groups. The topic of informal e-learning is covered in Chapter 10 in the sections on professional networks and communities of practice.

Table 9.1 Three forms of e-learning
Note: adapted from Mason (2002)

Web-based interactive learning packages	Online collaborative learning	Informal e-learning
Content-focused	Learner-focused	Group-focused
Delivery-driven	Activity-driven	Practice-driven
Individual learning	Small-group learning	Organizational learning
Minimal interaction with tutor	Significant interaction with tutor	Participants act as learners and tutors
No collaboration with other learners	Considerable interaction with other learners	Multi-way interactions among participants

What are the benefits and disadvantages of e-learning? There are many benefits in e-learning:

- Flexible delivery means learners can choose their place and time of study. The internet and world wide web are open 24 hours a day.

- Interactive learning resources can be relatively easily developed using a variety of standard packages.
- It can make use of, and link into, other resources available on the internet.
- Online delivery is relatively cheap as there are no printing or distribution costs.
- Flexible communications mean learners, tutors and information workers can communicate both in real time and asynchronously. It can bring together people from across the globe.
- It can enable both one-to-one and also one-to-many communications, e.g. tutor and individual learner, and tutor and whole groups.
- Learners can form both formal and informal learning communities.
- It doesn't have the negative associations often associated with formal educational settings.
- It is easy to track learner activity and progress.

However, there are also some major disadvantages of e-learning:

- Many people find it daunting, especially at first.
- The learner and tutor need reliable access to a computer and the internet.
- The learner and tutor need basic information technology skills.
- Training is required for both the tutor and learner.
- The development of high-quality learning materials is time consuming and expensive.
- Online tutoring can be more time consuming than face-to-face tutoring.
- Learning is a social process and many people enjoy face-to-face interactions.
- The use of the large virtual learning environments is expensive and may demand additional equipment and specialized workers.
- Some learning environments require state-of-the-art computers and the most up-to-date browser.

Web-based interactive learning packages

In the context of information and library work, web-based interactive learning packages are often used to deliver training courses in IT skills, information searching skills and also training in specific products and services, e.g. http://training.dialog.com. A useful list of tutorials is available at www.ics.ltsn.ac.uk/ILS/informationskillstutorials.html.

Today a variety of software tools makes it relatively easy (although still very time consuming) to develop interactive learning packages involving text, graphics, audio, video and animation. The best examples of interactive learning packages are based on sound ideas about learning and:

- arouse the learner's interest, e.g. through use of welcoming text, video clips, talking heads

- use language the learner can understand
- structure the content for ease of learning and provide a variety of routes through the materials
- explain difficult ideas or processes using simple language supported by clear images and diagrams
- give opportunities for learners to practise, e.g. quizzes, and give feedback.

The worst examples are those where traditional print-based materials are presented via the web or where trainers post their PowerPoint presentations and label them as examples of e-learning. This is rather like signing someone up for a dynamic training event and then sending them into a room with a procedures manual. Other bad examples provide an over-enthusiastic mixture of sound, vision and activities that can overwhelm the information worker (and also their PC). The development of high-quality interactive materials is an expensive process and many packages end up being underused or ignored. One essential element that is missing in this form of e-learning is the human touch: automated feedback, however positive, can come across as sterile and insincere. Many learners are hugely motivated by the social elements of learning and good feedback from their trainer.

Team leaders and supervisors may be involved in the use of web-based interactive learning packages as a training tool for themselves or team members. You may find that your organization provides access to a number of different e-learning training packages and these may be associated with training in the use of specialist computer systems such as the library circulation system or with common ICT packages, e.g. Microsoft Word or Microsoft Excel. Alternatively, you may find packages that are freely available over the internet that are relevant to your training needs. Many suppliers of databases or other resources provide access to web-based interactive learning packages too. You may find it helpful to use these packages for staff development within your team. If this is the case, then it is essential that you provide team members with 'protected time' so that they can use these packages without interruptions.

Collaborative learning in groups

The best training and development opportunities firmly place the learner at the centre and are focused on real-life issues and problems. Collaborative learning involves people coming together to work in small groups. It uses three main communication tools: discussion groups, conference or chat rooms, and e-mail for private communications. Good practice in the use of these tools is explored in Chapter 6.

Collaborative learning set in the context of universities or colleges tends to be focused on the use of virtual learning environments such as WebCT (www.WebCT. com) or Blackboard (www.Blackboard.com). Typically these systems offer a range of learning and teaching tools and resources, and these might include: dissemination of interactive multimedia learning resources; online assessment including diagnostic tools and tests; access to a wide range of information resources; e-mail; noticeboards; discussion groups; conference or chat rooms; personal management tools, e.g. diary, address book; online portfolio; learner management tools, e.g. monitoring of activity (number of log-ins, number of messages posted by individual learners), assessment results. Many universities, e.g. the University of Hull, offer information skills programmes using these facilities. Commercial organizations often use groupware such as Lotus Notes (www.LotusNotes.com) and this offers an extensive range of communication and knowledge-management tools. Information workers in the voluntary sector, solo workers and independent consultants or trainers often work with relatively small budgets and they can access free or very cheap community groupware, e.g. www.qub.ac.uk/mgt/itsoc/commnet.html and www.communities.org.uk.

Case study 9.2   Online learning for health librarians

FOLIO is a programme of online learning for health librarians in the UK. FOLIO forms part of the NeLH Librarian Development Programme which was established to provide support for librarians moving into new roles, focusing on the development of skills in health informatics and knowledge management, especially related to digital libraries. FOLIO was set up because librarians often find it difficult to get away from the workplace to attend training, whether because of staff shortages, limited budgets, travel time or other difficulties. FOLIO provides an opportunity for online learning that involves participants in engaging in a wide variety of learning activities, e.g. reading, focused activities, working with peers, support from facilitator(s), use of a website and also e-mail, use of communication tools such as a discussion groups, use of podcasts supporting PowerPoint presentations, and it involves a buddy system. More information is available at http://dev.nelh.nhs.uk/folio/.

While interactive learning packages are best suited for learning hard facts or rule-based procedural knowledge, collaborative learning is often closely linked with working on real-life complex problems. This makes it ideal for information workers to work collectively on common problems or issues relevant to their day-to-day work. Collaborative e-learning enables information workers to collaborate and learn from each other in the context of a structured and supportive environment, e.g. within the context of a masters programme. It is also widely used in communities of practice that are explored in Chapter 10.

Finally, while e-learning and teaching is unlikely to replace face-to-face training and education it is rapidly becoming an important additional delivery method and it offers opportunities to some people that are not readily available by any other means. E-learning means team leaders can offer their team members opportunities and also take opportunities themselves to develop new skills and knowledge in a flexible manner and one that suits the individual's work/life balance. It is a rapid growth area and one that is increasingly having an impact on information workers and the information profession.

Coaching

Coaching is a useful means of enhancing performance in the workplace. The idea of coaching is widely used in the worlds of sport and the arts where individuals may require coaching to help them to improve their skills and techniques. Coaching sessions can be set up in the workplace as part of an agreement between individuals who want to improve their performance and someone who has the necessary skills to be able to coach them.

Coaching sessions focus on developing specific set of skills such as:

- communication skills, e.g. the ability to give feedback, presentation skills, dealing with difficult situations
- technical skills, e.g. carrying out information searches on a variety of online sources, media skills such as video editing
- trainer skills, e.g. starting and ending group sessions, managing interventions.

A good coach is someone who is positive, enthusiastic, supportive, trusting, focused, goal-oriented, knowledgeable, observant, respectful, patient, clear and assertive. A coach will bring these skills together and use them appropriately throughout a coaching session. Individual coaching sessions can be planned using the learning and training plan outline presented earlier in this chapter.

It is important that individual sessions have the following characteristics as this will help them to be successful:

- clear aim and learning outcome
- clear structure which may take the form:
  — agreement of aim and learning outcomes
- team leader explains:
  — why a particular activity or issue is important
  — the required procedure or behaviour
- team leader models and demonstrates the required behaviour
- learner practises and:
  — is motivated to learn
  — responds positively to feedback
  — is very active in the coaching session
- team leader provides:
  — abundant detailed feedback
  — an emphasis throughout on learning and continuous improvement
  — reflection on practice and learning
- session ends on a positive note:
  — summary of learning achieved
  — identification of an action plan
  — arrangements made for next session (if appropriate)
  — individuals thank each other.

Whetherly gives the following example of a coaching process:

A coach is preparing to train a new library assistant on the computer issue system. To make the session most effective the coach will need to consider such factors as the knowledge and experience the library assistant has of such systems, what might be covered in the session and how the contents will be ordered, and also the date, time and venue, intervals between coaching, any necessary administrative arrangements, how the session will be reviewed, and what needs to be prepared in advance. Assuming a computer terminal is set up, the session may proceed as follows. The task is introduced and demonstrated to the learner, who is asked to explain it in her/his own words and then practise. When the learner has practised sufficiently the coach might demonstrate at full speed and ask her/him to try again. All this might be related appropriately to another aspect of using the system . . . time and many skills are required in the coach. One key skill is the ability to give feedback on how the learner is performing, which will enable him/her to have a sense of progress – 'You are accurate at this stage though you are not fast enough. You are following the procedure in the correct order'. To reiterate, effective coaching is greatly dependent on the skills of the coach.   Whetherly (1994)

Reflection

Reflection involves questioning, criticism, analysis and evaluation either during or at the end of a workplace learning activity or an event that takes place at work, e.g. incident with a reader, challenging query. Reflection is an essential activity in all workplace learning activities; it enhances learning and it is an essential part of CPD. Reflection can be introduced by team leaders into both team meetings and one-to-one meetings. It involves asking questions such as:

- What went well?
- What could be improved?
- What have you learnt?
- What would you do differently next time?

Building reflective activities into the structure of your workplace learning activities will help to ensure their success. See Case study 9.3

Case study 9.3   Reflection after a fire drill
There was a fire drill in a large government library and the library received criticism for not getting readers out of the building quickly enough. The criticism focused on the reading room and, in particular, the needs of readers with limited mobility. As a result of this criticism the reading room services staff spent time in their next team meeting reviewing what had worked well and what didn't work so well. They identified strategies

Table 9.2   Supporting reflection in workplace learning activities

Allocating time to reflect	The process of reflection is often squeezed out of everyday learning activities when busy team leaders or trainers are keen to include a lot of content. It is essential to allocate time for reflection. This time may be allocated during or at the end of a project, team meeting or learning activity. Time for reflection needs to be built into the workplace learning activities so that it is seen as an integral part of the learning process rather than a bolt-on extra.
Allocating space	The physical environment is also important if meaningful reflection is to take place. A quiet and non-distracting environment is important if team members are to focus on their findings in a thoughtful manner.
Developing psychological space	Team members need to feel psychologically comfortable and, in particular, confident and unthreatened if they are to be able to work reflectively in a meaningful manner. Some kinds of reflection, e.g. on issues such as career development, may raise emotional issues.
Questions that prompt reflection	Pre-prepared sets of questions may be used to prompt reflection. These could be very simple questions such as: why, what, how, what if?
Using questions to encourage a change of focus	Questions may also be used to help the learner to develop their perspective on a particular subject or activity. Typical questions may ask learners to change their focus from: a very detailed analysis to a broad picture (or *vice versa*) identifying similarities to identifying differences (or *vice versa*) self to others (or *vice versa*) the people to the task (or *vice versa*) content to process (or *vice versa*).
Capturing ideas	Ideas can be written down on flipchart paper, A4 paper or even Post-it™ notes. Many people keep learning logs and diaries and these are described in more detail by Moon (1999). Alternative forms of recording reflective practice may include the use of tools such as mind maps or media such as audio tapes or video.
Model reflective behaviour	Modelling reflective behaviour will help team members to incorporate reflection into their everyday work activities. Team leaders may: • reflect aloud on the learning process • refer back to a previous session in a reflective manner • ask for feedback as a means of explicitly reflecting on a particular activity/event/issue • reflect and ask for comment on their own performance and practice.

for improving their response rate and discussed how to deal with fire (and bomb) alarms at different times of the day when there were different levels of staffing. They came up with an action plan. The team leader discussed the action plan with the health and safety officer who gave it his approval. The team leader then spent some time explaining the fire/bomb emergency evacuation plan to the team. At the next fire drill, the library was praised for its rapid response and the way in which all the staff enabled the library to be evacuated within the target time.

The literature on reflection often refers to reflection-in-action (Schon, 1987). Reflection-in-action is the process of reflecting while the learner is on task. It is a short-term activity and the findings may be used to improve the quality of the outcome of the task. Team leaders can encourage reflection-in-action as team members are working on everyday tasks and activities, and also when they are taking part in workplace learning activities.

Reflection can be encouraged during day-to-day activities or specific workplace learning activities by team leaders providing an environment that supports reflection and this is outlined in Table 9.2 on the previous page.

Summary

This chapter has highlighted the importance of workplace learning and the need for team leaders to be pro-active and manage this process within their team. Understanding the ways in which the organization or ILS plans and supports learning and training activities is essential if you are to enable your team to grow and develop. In addition, encouraging and supporting learning and reflection in the workplace is likely to mean that you and your team learn from everyday events and activities within the ILS and this provides the basis for continuous improvement.

References

Kreber, C. (2005) Charting a Critical Course on the Scholarship of University Teaching Movement, *Studies in Higher Education*, **30** (4), 389–405.

Mason, R. (2002) Review of E-learning for Education and Training, *Networked Learning, 2002, proceedings of the third international conference, Sheffield University, 26–28 March 2002*, 19–26.

Moon, J. (1999) *Learning Journals*, London, Kogan Page.

Schon, D. (1987) *Educating the Reflective Practitioner*, San Francisco CA, Jossey-Bass.

Whetherly, J. (1994) *Management of Training and Staff Development*, London, Library Association Publishing.

10 Personal and professional development

Introduction

The purpose of this chapter is to explore practical approaches to personal growth and development. This is vital if you are to provide effective team leadership or supervision particularly if you are working in a challenging and turbulent environment. Individuals who are effective team leaders and supervisors are often very clear about who they are and what they want to get out of their work as well as other aspects of their lives. They are likely to pay attention to the topics covered in this chapter which include looking after yourself; work/life balance; time management; personal and career support; professional networks and communities of practice; and personal portfolios.

Looking after yourself

Team leaders and supervisors are likely to experience a range of challenges in the workplace, e.g. demanding workload, information overload, initiative overload, issues arising from individual team members or customers, new ways of working in a team, new working practices and/or technical innovations. As a result it is important to be able to manage yourself in the workplace so that you can lead your team in a relatively stress-free manner.

Key aspects of looking after yourself in the workplace may include:

- Know your own work peaks and troughs. Most people have times of the day when they are full of energy and other times when their energy is low. For example some people are at their best in the morning (larks) while others are afternoon or evening people (owls). If you know your best times and you are able to organize when you carry out your work then it makes sense to do your most demanding work when your energy levels are at their highest.
- Have tea breaks and lunch breaks. Eat healthy food.
- When you have a break, if possible get away from your desk and get some fresh air.
- Keep your working environment clean, tidy and uncluttered (see Chapter 5).
- Use time-management techniques (see summary in Figure 10.1).
- Speak to colleagues if you feel overwhelmed.
- Use breaks to network with colleagues.

One important way of looking after yourself is to manage your work/life balance and this important topic is considered in the next session.

Managing your work/life balance

Many of the changes in work and society that are outlined in Chapter 1 are linked to what is sometimes called the acceleration and compression of time and space. For example, while working on this chapter today I received an e-mail from a colleague in China and I was able to reply to him within five minutes after consulting with another colleague who is attending a conference in Ireland. This type of almost instant global communications across a number of countries would have been hard to imagine twenty years ago. Eriksen (2001) talks about 'fast time' and 'slow time'. Fast time is linked to the rise in information communications technology resulting in increased access to information at ever increasing speeds. This means that we are often bombarded at work with new initiatives, constant change and an ever-increasing flood of e-mails and other virtual communications. This can be an extremely stressful experience. Another effect of this fast time is that it replaces slow time which is required for certain kinds of emotional and intellectual experiences (Land, 2006). This is particularly relevant to team leaders who may be pressurized by fast time and not realize how important it is to build in time for reflection and workplace relationships. One of the main messages within this book is the importance of building in time for reflection and learning in our day-to-day working lives (see Chapter 9).

The concept of work/life balance has risen in importance in recent years; the term suggests that it is possible to develop a balance between work and the rest of our lives. It is linked with changes in society, including the move to a 24/7 global economy; changes in employment legislation, e.g. UK Employment Act 2002 and the European Working Time Directive 2003; and UK government reports on work/life balance promoting family-friendly policies and practices such as flexible working, maternity and paternity leave (Taylor, 2003). In addition, there is a health and safety argument for promoting work/life balance as someone whose life is well balanced is less likely to be taken ill due to stress. There are drivers in the workplace that help the work/life balance movement, e.g. it apparently helps reduce absenteeism; improves creativity and customer satisfaction; supports equal opportunity and diversity initiatives; promotes a healthier workforce; and enables organizations to demonstrate their integrity.

Different researchers emphasize different aspects of work/life balance. Clark (2002, 37) defines work/life balance as 'satisfaction and good functioning at work and at home, with a minimum of role conflict'; White et al. (2003) refer to work–family spill-over; while Sturges and Guest (2004) discuss work/non-work conflict. The concept is complex and involves the overlaps and interactions that may take place between life and work, and the conflicts and imbalances that may arise between different aspects of our lives.

Work/life balance is tackled at a number of different levels, e.g. by governments, through relevant legislation, by employers, by the trade union movement as well as by individuals. A wide range of options for promoting work/life balance is available and they include:

- annualized hours
- cafeteria benefits
- compressed working hours
- flexi-time
- gap year
- job-sharing
- sabbatical
- self-scheduling
- shift swapping
- staggered hours
- tele-working
- term-time working
- time off in lieu
- working from home.

The benefits of giving employees some control over their work/life balance are increased work satisfaction, greater commitment to the organization and their team, improved productivity, and increased retention of staff. However, there are some barriers to implementing work/life practices and these include understaffing, fears of loss of control over employee's working time, fears and resistance from team leaders and supervisors, potential damage to individual careers, and the organizational culture.

Within an organization the human resources department is likely to be responsible for introducing work/life balance policies and practices. Team leaders and managers within an ILS may be responsible for implementing them. At an individual level work/life balance practice involves asking people:

- What do you *want* from your work/life balance?
- How do you sort out conflicting demands on your time, physical energy and emotional energy?
- How do you achieve the self-discipline required to set boundaries and to say 'no'?
- How do you recognize and manage the stress that comes from conflicting or excessive demands (from work or home)?
- How can your team leader or supervisor support you in achieving your desired balance?

Introducing a work/life balance is a whole-organization activity and it needs to be part of the strategic plan and supported by senior managers. It also requires individual managers and team leaders to role-model the required behaviours and to implement relevant practices, e.g. flexi-time, shift swapping or working from home, in line with the organization's policies and practices.

Time management

Time management is an issue for many team leaders and it may be caused by a number of different reasons including:

- poor initial planning of the work
- underestimation of the time requirements of new tasks
- the team leader or supervisor and team being over-ambitious and taking on work that is not appropriately resourced
- lack of a clear agreement between the team leader and team members about the division of time between running an ILS and working on special projects
- individual staff being allocated too much work
- absence of key knowledge or skills.

The use of the routine work and project planning techniques outlined in Chapter 5 should help prevent time management issues arising as a result of the first five reasons. Staff training and development is essential if team leaders and their team are to be effective in their work and this is covered in Chapter 9. One special case is that of information and library workers who are involved in leading and working on multiple teams and projects (see Chapter 7), as they sometimes find that the demands of each of the teams and projects peak at the same time; if this coincides with a period of high demand from the information or library service then it can lead to an extremely stressful time. One important strategy to handle this situation is to manage the whole work schedule (everyday ILS work plus projects) as a series of linked projects: project management software such as MS Project provides tools that enable you to consolidate projects (see Chapter 5). Again, the issue may be avoided by detailed planning including risk analysis.

For those people for whom time management is an important issue there are many books to refer to (see Further reading at the end of this book). Figure 10.1 summarizes many of the current ideas and techniques for time management.

Activity: Where does my time go?

The purpose of this activity is to identify and reflect on the ways in which you spend your time at work. A useful starting point is to keep a detailed diary of all your workplace activities over a five-day period and then to classify them using the following scheme:

At regular times ask yourself: 'What is the best use of my time right now?'	**E-mails and phones** In some situations it is possible to limit use of e-mail to a few times per day. Flag up important e-mails. Use folder facility. Use voice mail. Axe membership of some discussion groups.
Enquiries Remember to use existing materials. Find out how much information is required. Keep a Frequently asked questions (FAQ) file. Remember that 20% of your effort will achieve 80% of the results (Pareto effect).	**Interruptions** Put a sign on your door or close the door. Negotiate with the enquirer and book a specific time to discuss the issue. Minimize interruptions when completing certain tasks, e.g. report writing Use a quiet room or space. Ask a colleague to answer your phone.
Meetings Put time limits on agenda items. Put time limits on meetings. Attend part of a meeting not a whole meeting. Hold meetings in rooms with no chairs. Have online rather than face-to-face meetings.	**Paper work** Use Post-it™ notes to highlight action. Use highlighter pens to mark out key information.
Post Sort your post into four groups: • priority – deal with it immediately • delegate to someone • hold; not important – work through once a week/fortnight when your energy level is low • useless: file in bin.	**Prioritize** Prioritize work by organizing it under the following four headings: • urgent and important • important but not urgent • urgent but not important • not urgent and not important. Alternatively items in your 'to do' list can be assigned priority based on these headings.
Self-management Know your own work peaks and troughs. Set your own calendar/schedule. Keep your desk clear. Have tea breaks and lunch breaks. Speak to colleagues if you feel overwhelmed. Use breaks to network with colleagues.	**Teamwork** Create and develop open working relationships. Give and receive support and feedback. Share difficult tasks.
Workloads Set realistic deadlines. Say 'no'. Set targets and rewards. Use a daily 'to do' list. Identify what you will achieve by the end of the day.	**Technology** Spend time learning how to use relevant packages. Attend relevant courses or workshops. Be selective in the use of technology, e.g. small projects are often best managed using paper and pen rather than MS Project.

Figure 10.1 Tips and techniques for time management

- urgent and important
- important but not urgent
- urgent but not important
- not urgent and not important.

You can then reflect on your findings. If you have a majority of 'urgent and important' activities then this indicates that you are working towards lots of deadlines and perhaps fire-fighting within your service. In this situation it may be worthwhile talking with your manager about the number of deadlines that you are facing. If you are spending too much time fire-fighting this can be indicative of an underlying problem. The problem-solving methodology introduced in Chapter 3 may be used to attempt to resolve this situation.

If you find that the majority of your activities are 'important but not urgent' this indicates that you are spending your time planning and preparing your work, or building up networks and relationships. People who find that they spend most of their time at work carrying out 'important but not urgent' tasks are often well organized and plan ahead. If you are experiencing problems with managing your time then it may be that your workload is too big.

Individuals who find that their time is made up of 'urgent but not important' tasks are likely to be busy but not achieve very much. It is possible that you are not delegating sufficient work to your team members. If you find that the majority of your work comes under this heading then you may find it helpful to review your work with your manager.

Finally if you find that you are spending more than 1% of your time on tasks that are 'not urgent and not important' then you have a major problem because you are unlikely to be fulfilling your role as a team leader or supervisor. You need to discuss your situation with your line manager as soon as possible.

Personal and career support

Many people find it helpful to create a network of support to help them manage the challenges of their work and also develop their career. Individual support networks are likely to be made up of a wide range of people including personal friends and family, current and past colleagues, your manager and a mentor (or mentors). An important means of gaining personal support is through mentoring which is 'learning by association with a role model'. Mentoring is an important way of gaining support in the following areas:

- moving from one role to another
- dealing with a specific issue or problem
- skills for a particular task or project
- training, support and development
- professional contacts and networks
- career and professional development.

Essentially a mentor is a friend and someone who will support your personal and career development. Some organizations have formal mentoring schemes which are typically aimed at new recruits or groups of staff who traditionally find barriers to their progression, e.g. women or staff from ethnic minorities. Informal mentoring schemes are very common and may be initiated by the person to be mentored, their line manager or a colleague. Typically an individual will identify a mentor within their own organization but some people, e.g. team leaders of small information services where there is an absence of more experienced library or information colleagues in their organization, may find it helpful to approach a colleague in another organization.

As a team leader it is worthwhile considering and possibly setting up a supportive mentoring process for yourself. Think about who may be able to act as your mentor and what you want to gain from the mentoring relationship. Some people work with more than one mentor, e.g. a team leader managing an information services team and also working on a new website project may work with two mentors, one for each aspect of their work. Typically mentoring involves meeting up with your mentor, e.g. at three-monthly intervals, and exploring your current situation and career plan. Sometimes mentoring takes place through a mixture of face-to-face and virtual communications. If you are seeking someone to mentor you as you progress from one role or project to another then it is important to choose a person with experience of that type of work and who remains up-to-date with new ideas and professional developments.

The mentoring process is likely to involve exploring issues and challenges, setting objectives, identifying an action plan, implementing the plan (which takes place outside of the mentoring process) and reflecting on the experience. These topics are covered in Chapters 5 and 9.

Working as a team leader, either leading a small team in a relatively stable environment or leading a multi-professional team, can be demanding and challenging. It is useful to have a mentor whom you can go to for help and support outside of the day-to-day line management processes within your organization. This may be someone within the profession who has had extensive experience of the particular type of information work and who may be working at a senior level within your own or another organization. The availability of someone who will give you time and space to explore your current issues and problems in confidence can be a vital source of support. It can also be a valuable source of career help and support as illustrated in Case study 10.1.

Case study 10.1　Mentoring

Helen Jamieson developed her career from that of a learning services supervisor to manager with the help and support of a management development programme (Black and Jamieson, 2005, 15). An intrinsic part of this programme was mentoring and Helen writes:

'Each participant was allocated a mentor for the duration of the programme – this mentor was a member of the senior management team and therefore an experienced member of learning services in terms of managing staff, teams and projects. My mentor was on hand to help guide me through the process, to be a confidante and a sounding board – but was also someone who could get me to think, develop, reflect and evaluate. Quite early on in the programme, my mentor and I agreed that one of my main priorities would be to look at service planning and development. We thought that this would enable me to start thinking and working at a more strategic level. As a result, I became involved in learning services' off-campus strategy group and started to feed into decisions and planning at a much higher level within the service.

I started the leaders and managers programme as supervisor in learning services. However, the enormous range of skills and experience that I gained throughout the programme gave me the confidence to apply for a secondment to a manager's position within the service. I am now four months into this new position, and I'm so glad that I was chosen to be part of the programme. It has given me a lot more confidence, a wide range of new skills, belief in my own ability and an insight into what managing staff, teams and projects is really all about. Since starting my new role I have already been involved in a wide variety of projects and new developments. Here I have been able to draw on the skills that I have developed throughout the programme. Learning services is presently in the process of developing various service areas including self-issue and other self-service developments – and I have gained the confidence to become involved in the development of these projects and take on a leadership role.'

Professional networks

Many information and library workers at all levels from library assistant to director gain information and support through becoming involved in local, regional, national or international networks. These networks offer a valuable support network to team leaders and supervisors as they enable you to make contact with and gain help from colleagues who are in a similar position to yourself. Many of these networks are established and maintained by professional associations such as the Chartered Institute for Library and Information Professionals (CILIP), the American Library Association (ALA) and the Australian Library and Information Association (ALIA). Membership fees vary and are often linked with salaries. However, the benefits of membership includes access to professional journals, access to specialist networks and groups, and discounted fees for training events or books. This section explores the following topics: education and training events, conferences and virtual communication tools.

Education and training events

Support, advice, training and development can be obtained through attending workshops or training events, or taking part in e-learning programmes (see Chapter 9). These may be organized by a professional association or a specialist information and library group. There are often regional or local groups that run training events too, e.g. Scottish Library and Information Council, British and Irish Association of Law Librarians, M62 Group. In addition, commercial organizations and information and library suppliers often provide training events. Large employing organizations run staff development workshops and these many be on general communication or management issues, or on the organization's policies and practices, e.g. selection and recruitment.

You may decide that you want to develop your knowledge and understanding of information and library work through a formal education programme, e.g. a degree or postgraduate degree. Alternatively, you may decide to develop your knowledge and skills in leadership, management and supervision by taking a recognized qualification in management, e.g. certificate in management or a management degree, or by taking part in a management and leadership programme frequently offered to employees of large organizations (see section on mentoring in this chapter). Nowadays there is a huge range of education programmes available for people who want to develop their knowledge and skills and obtain a qualification.

Conferences

The main value of conferences and conferencing is building, maintaining and developing your professional networks. Meeting up with old friends and colleagues in a variety of venues helps to establish working relationships. Professional updating is a standard reason for going to conferences; for individuals at the start of their career it is a useful way of gaining an overview of a topical theme or issue. For people who are active players in a field it can be a way of gaining valuable nuggets of information and exchanging ideas with others. In my experience the process of participating in a conference, whether it is attending presentations or workshops or chatting to people in the inevitable coffee queue, often sparks off new ideas and connections which lead to new approaches to tackling old problems on return to the workplace. The exhibitions that stand alongside the main conference activities often provide up-to-date information on a variety of information systems, as well as being a useful source of free pens, mugs and other novelties ranging from pots of honey to the inevitable mouse mat. For people working in an academic environment the process of presenting a paper at a conference and then subsequently gaining publication for it is a requirement of the job. The pressure on people to publish appears to be leading to a glut of papers of variable quality. However, presenting ideas to one's peers and gaining feedback is an extremely valuable way of improving and developing current practice whether or not it leads to publication.

Budgets for staff development and attending conferences are often tight and conference websites provide a useful way of catching up with current ideas without attending the conference. Many conference websites provide full access to conference papers and presentations (either during or soon after the close of the conference) and increasingly many give access to podcasts of keynote speakers and selected presentations.

The costs of physically attending conferences can be huge. Travel, hotel and registration fees all add up, sometimes to substantial sums of money. In addition our time away from the workplace is an additional cost to our employer. My own experience is that a huge amount of personal energy needs to be invested in successful conferencing – getting to know and talking with a wide range of people often for long hours each day can be exhausting.

Virtual conferences are becoming an important part of the conferencing world. Virtual conference fees are generally much cheaper than those for traditional ground-based conferences. How do you take part in a virtual conference? Many organizations now provide access to virtual conferencing environments and, like their ground-based equivalents (hotels and conference centres), they provide a range of facilities both before, during and after the conference. A vast range of activities takes place in the virtual conference sites and they may include keynote presentations, e.g. by narrated PowerPoint slides or podcasts; asynchronous discussions and real-time chat sessions; question and answer sessions; virtual café, syndicate rooms and breakout activities. My own experience is that these tend to work well and sometimes the biggest challenge is working out the time zones! High-quality technical support and the availability of a virtual technical help desk is vital. Icohere.com advertises the benefits of virtual conferences as:

- one-tenth the cost of traditional conferences
- easy access using a standard web browser and the MacroMedia Flash plug-in
- access through any firewall
- flexible event schedule – attend any time during the week
- downloadable presentations and practical resources
- connecting directly with experts
- networking with other attendees.

To conclude this section on conferences, what are the overall benefits of face-to-face and virtual conferences? The traditional conference where you meet and mingle with a diverse range of people seems to offer a richer experience than the virtual conference. There is something extremely valuable about actually meeting people and getting to know them through sharing a range of experiences – presentations, discussions, lunch, the coffee queue and the range of leisure activities organized by the conference committee. The conference ritual adds to our professional lives and provides a foundation of shared experiences, stories and jokes that then help to form the basis of many professional relationships. In contrast, the virtual conference sometimes feels extremely one dimensional and text-based, and although 'conversations' are often deep and intense it is sometimes difficult to understand where a particular participant is coming from. In addition to the lack of visual clues such as body language from other participants there is also a distinct absence of freebies!

Virtual communication tools

Nowadays many professional activities take place through virtual communication tools such as discussion lists, discussion groups or bulletin boards and weblogs. Virtual communication tools have become an important tool for continuous professional development. They are particularly useful for information and library workers who are isolated geographically or working as a solo information worker. They enable busy information and library workers to keep up to date and network with other professionals interested in the same theme or topic. They offer an important source of professional help and support.

Discussion lists

Discussion lists are also called mailing lists or list-servs. These different names refer to the same process in which you can send an e-mail to a large group of people rather like using the CC facility. The process is managed by a hosting service that maintains a list of all the different discussion lists and the people who subscribe to them. It is run using a mail server that is a piece of software that stores a mailing list of e-mail addresses to individuals. There are thousands of discussion lists (or mail lists) available on the internet, each devoted to a particular topic and aimed at a specific audience. Discussion lists can be used in a variety of ways and, in general, they provide a forum for:

- requests for factual information
- requests for advice and opinions or experiences
- information about new websites, products and publications
- assistance with software or hardware problems
- advice on buying or using new systems
- conference and meeting announcements
- staff development announcements
- information about vacancies.

The advantages and disadvantages of discussion lists are presented in Table 10.1. Information about discussion lists is available from a number of sources including professional associations such as CILIP (see www.cilip.org.uk) which provides a wide range of online discussion groups for its members including Diversity, European Programmes, School Librarians' Network and Voluntary Sector Information Workers. They are available at www.cilip.org.uk/professional guidance/discussion/. The

Table 10.1 Advantages and disadvantages of discussion lists

Advantages	Disadvantages
Quick and easy method of communication	Can be difficult to separate out facts from opinions
Provides access to wide group of people	Can waste a lot of time, e.g. reading irrelevant messages
Speedy response – sometimes within minutes!	May be overwhelmed by e-mails
Good method of keeping up to date	Discussions may be on very specific topics and not relevant to your particular interests
Good method of tapping into practical experience and expertise	List may be dominated by a few people
Good method of networking	Personal disputes may dominate or sour discussion list
Based on e-mail doesn't require specialist software	

American Library Association (see www.ala.org/) has more than 254 lists on a wide range of topics including Adult Literacy Library Initiatives, Grass-roots America and Women's Studies Section. E-mail discussion lists are available for different groups of ILS staff across the world. Some groups may be focused on a relatively small interest area, e.g. the Web4Lib electronic discussion is for the discussion of issues relating to the creation, management and support of library-based world wide web servers, services and applications (see http://lists.webjunction.org/web4lib/).

Discussion groups or bulletin boards

These were introduced in Chapter 6 and they provide an opportunity for online debate and discussion. Discussion or e-mail lists work by sending e-mails to all subscribers to the list. This means that the e-mail arrives on your desktop. In contrast, discussion groups or bulletin boards are located on an internet site, e.g. as part of a virtual learning environment, or are part of an organizational intranet site. This means that you have to access the site yourself to view and respond to the latest messages. Many systems provide e-mail notification of the arrival of new discussion group messages.

Discussion groups or bulletin boards may be open or closed. An example of open discussion groups is available at the award-winning FreePint website site at www.freepint.com/. Many professional groups or organizations set up discussion groups as part of development programmes or activities, or are associated with projects or new initiatives. These groups provide an online space where members may discuss their work, share ideas and work together in an online environment. They are commonly used by educational programmes as a means of letting students and tutors work together, and also project and virtual teams. These closed discussion groups provide an opportunity for individuals to work together in a confidential environment (see Case study 10.2). They form the basis of many virtual communities of practice and these are explored later in this chapter.

Case study 10.2   Consultation within an academic library
One academic library in central England set up a discussion group to enable
information and library workers to comment on and discuss proposals for a change in
ILS structure. Staff were able to post messages either under their own name or
anonymously. At the end of the consultation process individuals said they welcomed the
opportunity to give feedback on the proposals and they wanted discussion groups to be
used in future to enable discussion on important themes or issues. A number of staff said
they found it difficult to speak up in large meetings or in front of senior managers and
they liked the discussion group because it gave them time to think about and write their
comments in a non-stressful manner.

Weblogs

Another online communication tool is a weblog or blog – a frequently updated web-
page on a specific topic. They are normally established by enthusiastic individuals
or organizations, e.g. the BBC, who update their blogs at regular (sometimes
hourly) intervals. The structure of weblogs varies but typically they are divided into
two columns: one used for regular entries which appear in date order (most recent
first) and the second providing links to relevant sites. Many blogs provide a link
to enable readers to comment on the entries. This means that online discussions
build up over time and these sometimes provide useful comments and at other times
more helpful links or resources.

The Information Literacy weblog provided by Sheila Webber and Student Boon
is available at http://information-literacy.blogspot.com/. Phil Bradley's weblog is
focused on internet searching, web design, search engine development and other
technology-based developments that are relevant to librarians and information workers (see http://philbradley.typepad.com/). Both of these examples are very useful
for anyone who wants to keep up to date in these areas and I find that they often
provide access to information that is easily missed. An international list of weblogs
is available at www.libdex.com/weblogs.html.

Communities of practice

Professional networks such as discussion lists are examples of communities of interest and they are a very good means of gaining information. Another way in which
individual team leaders or supervisors can develop themselves and gain support is
by becoming a member of a community of practice. Table 10.2 on the next page
illustrates the differences between communities of interest and practice.

What is a community of practice? A simple definition of 'community' is that it
is a group of people who share a common interest or a common purpose. A community of practice is more complex than this because it involves people coming
together to share and develop collective knowledge, and translate this knowledge
into improved working and professional practices. This isn't a new idea and it can

Table 10.2 Comparison of communities of interest and communities of practice

Characteristics	Community of interest	Community of practice
Purpose	To be informed	To create, expand and share knowledge. To develop individual's professional practice.
Membership	People who become subscribers or members of a particular group, e.g. mail list, e-learning programme. Membership may be very large, e.g. 12–1000.	People who share a particular interest or passion in a topic. People who become subscribers or members of a particular group, e.g. mail list, e-learning programme. This may be self-selected or by invitation. Membership is likely to be relatively small, e.g. 6–24.
What holds them together?	Access to information and sense of community.	Passion, commitment, identity with group. Personal relationships within the group.
Examples in information and library profession	Some discussion groups, newsgroups.	Some groups involved in collaborative project work. Professional groups supported by professional organizations.

be tracked back through time. For example, in the Middle Ages the instinct to collaborate and share good practice was harnessed and communities were formed to support the collective development of specialist trades and practices, e.g. the Guild of Musicians. Members of a community of practice may communicate with each other through meetings, conferences or virtual tools, e.g. e-mail, bulletin boards or chat rooms. A major impetus to research and thinking about work-based communities was the publication by Jean Lave and Etienne Wenger (1991) of their seminal book *Situated Learning: legitimate peripheral participation*. Lave and Wenger adopted the phrase 'community of practice' and proposed that learning is an integral part of the process of participation in a community and that it cannot be separated from the social situation and interactions through which it occurs. Wenger et al. defined a 'community of practice' as:

> groups of people who share a concern, a set of problems, or a passion about a topic,
> and who deepen their knowledge and expertise in this area by interacting on an
> ongoing basis.   Wenger et al. (2002, 4)

What are the benefits of joining a community of practice? Communities of practice are an important means by which individuals can discuss real-life issues and gain new insights, potential solutions or strategies. These professional groups are particularly important in enabling individuals and groups to identify and explore current issues and problems, particularly those that are on the boundaries of accepted knowledge. They offer a means through which individuals and groups construct new knowledge and develop approaches to tackling current problems. They also offer a way in which new members to the profession gain access to experience, ideas and professional support. Communities of practice can also support inter-professional collaboration, e.g. I am a member of a small community of practice made up of information and library workers, IT experts, academics and educational developers. Some of the benefits of membership of a community of practice include:

- access to information and expertise
- access to like-minded individuals
- opportunity to find innovative solutions to complex problems
- sense of identity and group membership
- support and friendship
- opportunity to 'let off steam' in a safe environment
- confidence building and professional expertise.

Involvement in communities of practice also brings benefits to the library or information unit. Wenger et al. (2002) identify short- and long-term benefits which are summarized in Table 10.3.

Table 10.3 Benefits of membership of a community of practice

Short-term benefits	Long-term benefits
<ul><li>quick answers to questions</li><li>opportunities to discuss specific issues</li><li>improved quality of decisions</li><li>wider perspective on problems and issues</li><li>possibilities for sharing resources</li><li>continuing professional development of those involved</li><li>increased productivity</li><li>increased levels of practitioner competence</li><li>ability to take risks with backing of the community.</li></ul>	<ul><li>service improvements</li><li>forum for 'benchmarking' against other information or library units</li><li>ability to establish long-term relationships with colleagues and other ILS services</li><li>ability to act as a pressure group</li><li>opportunities for collaboration on projects</li><li>opportunities to share resources</li><li>ability to take advantage of emerging opportunities</li><li>emergence of unplanned capabilities and opportunities.</li></ul>

Communities of practice may exist as face-to-face, virtual or blended communities where members may meet together or communicate using online tools. Some of the benefits of membership of a virtual community of practice are expressed by Hyams and Mezey, who write:

virtual communities offer much richer opportunities to share best practice and know-how in an active sense. They can stimulate the sharing of intelligence, and make it possible to harvest, organize and share 'knowledge' for preservation and re-use. They provide common ground for solving problems and sharing insights . . . Communities offer much more than mere email discussion lists to members, too, because they can share access to resources (including multimedia and datasets), and communicate in real time using facilities such as live chat.   Hyams and Mezey (2003, 36)

Who benefits from membership of communities of practice? Evaluations of communities of practice demonstrate that they are particularly helpful for three groups (Lewis and Allan, 2004):

- New entrants to a profession who are managing the challenges of establishing their own professional credibility and translating and applying academic theory into practice. Communities of practice can provide newly qualified professionals with ready access to established practitioners' knowledge and experience offering a safe environment in which to model and observe professional practice.
- Individuals who are moving into situations that are new to them, e.g. as a result of a change in employment in which they want to quickly develop relevant knowledge and expertise.
- Individuals who are working at the forefront of specialist knowledge and tackling new problems and unique situations. Communities of practice provide them with access to experienced colleagues with whom they can discuss and construct knowledge and develop new approaches to practice.

This means that they are particularly relevant to new team leaders and supervisors, and also individuals facing new or innovative workplace situations.

How do you join a community of practice? Many communities of practice are advertised in the ILS literature and on the websites of professional associations. Some spring up spontaneously, e.g. when like-minded people meet at conferences or other events. Participating in communities of practice fosters professional development by providing a forum for expanding skills and expertise, and enabling individual information workers to keep up to date. Membership of communities of practice can also lead to enhanced professional reputation and so increased marketability and employability. Information workers who are members are likely to develop a strong sense of professional identity and this is particularly important to relatively new entrants to the field and also people who are working in solo libraries or information units.

What happens within a community of practice? As with any group or team, communities of practice experience a life cycle; they often go through the following development stages (rather like the team development process covered in Chapter 2):

- decision to join the community
- socialization
- tentative working together
- productive working together
- closure/moving on.

The decision to join a community involves identifying, exploring and discussing the community goals. It involves answering questions such as: Why am I here? Do I want to commit time to this community? Will this community provide me with what I currently want and need? Do I want to become involved with these people? The initial socialization is rather like that at a party – a little awkward at the start, but once the ice is broken (and this may be facilitated by a virtual café) then great fun. Members may come from all around the world and share a common interest, a desire to improve professional practice and also a willingness to socialize. Initial online working is often very tentative and everyone is on their best behaviour and demonstrating their best manners. This quickly moves on to positive, powerful and productive working together as a group.

Different people are likely to participate at different levels within a community. Wenger et al. (2002) identify three levels: peripheral members who rarely participate but are on the sidelines observing discussions; active members (who join in with discussions when they feel they have something to say); and core members who introduce new topics or projects, and help shape and lead the community. Wenger et al. (2002) suggest that there is a personal development route from being peripheral through to becoming an active or core member. Many information workers will be familiar with this model even if they have not previously conceptualized it in these terms. It is a model that appears to operate in traditional face-to-face professional groups, e.g. special interest groups of AALA, ALA or CILIP. In virtual groups, as in more traditional professional groups, the presence of a coordinator or facilitator can help integrate new members into the community and this will enable them to become active or core members. Again like the face-to-face support groups, in virtual environments the use of e-buddies can be a useful means of providing support and encouragement to new community members.

Finally, the community has completed its work and the reason for working together in a community may have come to an end. Some communities fizzle out while others take time and attention to close the community. In some cases group members may decide to move forward, capitalize on their ability to work in a productive community, and develop new goals and *raisons d'être*. They then establish a new or redefined community and the cycle starts again.

Personal portfolios

Chapters 9 and 10 consider workplace learning and personal and professional development. It is likely that as a team leader and supervisor you will be involved in a wide range of formal and informal development processes and activities. There is a danger that this learning process is submerged in the day-to-day activities in the workplace. One approach to capturing and recording these activities is through a personal portfolio. A personal portfolio is a record of your achievements. It may include a variety of entries including:

- contents page
- *curriculum vitae*
- personal development plan
- certificates and qualifications
- evidence of attendance at conferences or courses
- letters of thanks or congratulations
- a learning journal
- photographs
- newspaper or professional journal articles.

Personal portfolios may be kept as a printed version, e.g. in an A4 file, or as an electronic portfolio. Professional associations such as CILIP may recommend and support the use of personal portfolios as a means of supporting continuous professional development. In this case you may be provided with specific guidance as to how to develop your portfolio. Some organizations support their use while many individuals find that they are valuable tools for personal growth and development.

Personal portfolios may be used as a record of personal and professional development for use in:

- applying for membership of a professional association
- applying for promotion (both in completing an application form and also preparing for an interview)
- applying to go on a degree or higher degree programme
- reflecting on and discussing your future career path with your mentor or line manager
- reviewing your achievements to raise your self-confidence or to feel good about yourself and your work.

Summary

This chapter highlights the importance of managing yourself and your own professional development. This involves looking after yourself; work/life balance; time management; personal and career support, e.g. through mentoring. The chapter emphasizes the importance of taking part in professional networks and communities of practice. For all information and library team leaders and supervisors there is extensive support available either face-to-face or through virtual channels and this provides a means of continuous professional development. Finally, I strongly recommend that you keep a personal portfolio as it will help you to integrate and develop your workplace activities and your career. A personal portfolio provides a valuable record of your work, your achievements and successes, and it enables you to identify your strengths and also areas for development.

References

Black, C. and Jamieson, H. (2005) I'm New to Management – get me out of here, *SCONUL Focus*, (36), 14–16.

Clark, S. C. (2002) Communicating Across the Work/Home Border, *Community, Work and Family*, **5** (1), 747–70.

Eriksen, T. H. (2001) *Tyranny of the Moment: fast and slow time in the information age*, London, Pluto.

Hyams, E. and Mezey, M. (2003) Virtuous Virtual, *Library and Information Update*, **2** (1), 36–7.

Land, R. (2006) Networked Learning and the Politics of Speed: a dromological perspective, *Networked Learning 2006*, Lancaster, University of Lancaster, www.networkedlearningconference.org.uk/ [accessed 21 June 2006].

Lave, J. and Wenger, E. (1991) *Situated Learning: legitimate peripheral participation*, Cambridge, Cambridge University Press.

Lewis, D. and Allan, B. (2004) *Virtual Learning Communities*, Maidenhead, Open University Press.

Sturges, J. and Guest, D. (2004) Working to Live or Living to Work?, *Human Resource Management Journal*, **14** (4), 5–21.

Taylor, R. (2003) *The Future of Work-Life Balance*, ESRC, www.leeds.ac.uk/esrcfutureofwork/ downloads/fow_publication_2.pdf [accessed 31 January 2005].

Wenger, E., McDermott, R. and Snyder, W. M. (2002) *Cultivating Communities of Practice: a guide to managing knowledge*, Boston MA, Harvard Business School Press.

White, M., Hill, S., McGovern, P., Mills, C. and Smeaton, D. (2003) High Performance Management Practices, Working Hours and Work-life Balance, *British Journal of Industrial Relations*, **41** (2), 175–95.

Further reading

Allan, B. (2002) *E-learning and Teaching in Library and Information Services*, London, Facet Publishing.

Allan, B. (2004) *Project Management: tools and techniques for today's ILS professional*, London, Facet Publishing.

Bray, T. and Simpson, T. (2006) *A Manager's First 100 Days*, London, CIPD.

Clutterbuck, D. (2004) *Everyone Needs a Mentor*, 4th edn, London, CIPD.

Clutterbuck, D. and Megginson, D. (2005) *Making Coaching Work*, London, CIPD.

Corrall, S. (2000) *Strategic Management of Information Services*, London, ASLIB/IMI.

Currie, D. (2006) *Introduction to Human Resource Management*, London, CIPD.

Curzon, S. C. (2006) *Managing Change: a how-to-do-it manual for librarians*, London, Facet Publishing.

de Sáez, E. E. (2002) *Marketing Concepts for Libraries and Information Services*, 2nd edn, London, Facet Publishing.

Hackett, P. (2003) *Training Practice*, London, CIPD.

Jackson, M. (2003) *Systems Thinking: creative holism for managers*, Chichester, Wiley.

Jackson, T. (2000) *Career Development*, London, CIPD.

Larson, C. E. and Lafasto, F. M. J. (1989) *Teamwork*, London, Sage.

Massis, B. E. (2003) *The Practical Library Manager*, Binghamton NY, Haworth Press.

Megginson, D. and Whitaker, V. (2003) *Continuous Professional Development*, London, CIPD.

Melling, M. and Little, J. (eds) (2002) *Building a Successful Customer-service Culture: a guide for library and information managers*, London, Facet Publishing.

Metz, R. F. (2001) *Coaching in the Library: a management strategy for achieving excellence*, Chicago, American Library Association.

Pantry, S. and Griffiths, P. (2000) *Developing a Successful Service Plan*, London, Facet Publishing.

Pantry, S. and Griffiths, P. (2003) *Your Essential Guide to Career Success*, 2nd edn, London, Facet Publishing.

Pantry, S. and Griffiths, P. (2005) *Setting up a Library and Information Service from Scratch*, London, Facet Publishing.

Parsloe, E. (1999) *The Manager as Coach and Mentor*, 2nd edn, London, CIPD.

Pearn, M. (1998) *Empowering Team Learning*, London, CIPD.

Pugh, L. (2000) *Change Management in Information Services*, Aldershot, Gower.

Roberts, S. and Rowley, J. (2004) *Managing Information Services*, London, Facet Publishing.

Sheldrick Ross, C. and Dewdney, P. (1998) *Communicating Professionally: a how-to-do-it manual for library applications*, 2nd edn, London, Facet Publishing.

Winstanley, D. (2005) *Personal Effectiveness*, London, CIPD.

Index